S0-DFH-501

# How to Grow an Adventist Church

## RUSSELL BURRILL

**HART BOOKS**
A Ministry of Hart Research Center
Fallbrook, California

Copyright © 2009 by Hart Research Center
Printed in the United States of America
All Rights Reserved

Editing and page design by Page One Communications
Cover art direction and design by Ed Guthero
Cover illustration by Chang Park

ISBN: 978-1-878046-69-7

# Contents

# Introduction

The heart of every pastor and the passion of every church member should be to see their church grow and become what God desires their church to be. Yet that passion often becomes lost in the attempt to accomplish the mission of Jesus. Jesus commanded us, in Matthew 28:16-20, to go and make disciples. Yet many times it seems we would rather argue about how we should make disciples than to actually go forth and do what Jesus commanded.

Throughout the course of my ministry, I have seen countless churches hopelessly divided over the issue of church growth. Arguments have broken out as to what is the best method to evangelize. We end up pitting one method against each other, while we sit back and do nothing. How pleased the enemy must be.

It is not a question of numerical growth or spiritual growth. The church needs both. It is not a question of who originated the method—if it works and is in harmony with biblical standards, use it. What constantly amazes me is that those who criticize church growth so often are doing nothing. I would be the first to admit that our methods are not perfect, but until we find something better, let's not kick out what *is* working for us as Adventists.

Some, in their attempt to find answers, have swarmed to the latest church growth conferences offered by some non–Adventist agency. Then they bring back those methods and attempt to implement them in their little Adventist church, only to be disappointed. Not all the methods used by other churches are usable in the Adventist setting. There are some unique things about the way Adventists evangelize that do not work for other groups, but do work for us. That is why this book is entitled, *How to Grow an **Adventist** Church.* Many principles from the church growth movement can be easily accommodated in Adventism and found useful. We will notice some of them in this book, but there are other issues not covered in church growth literature that are essential for Adventist growth. We must explore them as well. We must develop a discriminating mind as we search through the vast amount of material that has been written about church growth.

It would be most helpful for each person to be thoroughly immersed in the excellent counsel given to this church by Ellen White. The principles of growth are all found there. As we study church growth literature, we will discover numerous methodologies. We need to compare them to those basic principles given this movement through the prophetic gift. In that way we will learn what will work in the Adventist context.

In this book, we will survey some basic information from church growth literature that is applicable to Adventists. The most crucial chapter in the book is the second, where we discuss the culture of evangelism. This chapter, I believe, is worth the price of the whole book. When what is discussed in chapter two is put into action, any methodology will work.

I hope you enjoy this work, but even more so, I hope you begin putting it into action immediately, especially chapter 2. It is my prayer that the passion of reaching the lost will once more grip Adventist churches around the world. May our churches truly be Adventist. In my understanding, they cannot be Adventist unless they are reaching out for lost people. That is the heart of our mission, the heart of Adventism. May it happen in your church now.

Russell Burrill
Berrien Springs, Michigan
April, 2009

# CHAPTER ONE

# The Challenge of the Unreached

Pastor Matt had struggled for some time with the lack of growth in the Browning Seventh-day Adventist Church. He held evangelistic meetings periodically, and even though there were always baptisms, attendance at church did not seem to vary. He was becoming more and more concerned about the vast number of unreached people in the vicinity of the church and the lack of concern displayed by his church members.

He felt it was time for change. His own life had recently been challenged by the friendships he had made among unchurched people in his community. He was very concerned because of the attitudes of the unchurched toward Christians. They told him that they could relate to him because he was different—not like the other Christians. When Matt pressed them as to what they meant, his friends finally admitted that they really did not know any Christians, but from what the media projected, they knew they did not like Christians.

If the unchurched made judgments about Christians based on the media, Matt knew that Christian believers were in trouble. He felt a sermon erupting deep in his soul. Next Sabbath he preached a powerful sermon on the need for Adventists to make contacts and become friends with the unchurched people in their community. He wanted to break through this barrier of misunderstanding so that the unchurched would discover the positive things about genuine Christianity.

John is considered one of the faithful members of the Browning Seventh-day Adventist Church, located in a major American city. He attends church weekly, serves the church as a deacon, and once in awhile teaches an adult Sabbath School class. His wife, Sue, is involved with the Kindergarten Sabbath School, and both their boys are active in Pathfinders. Their lives revolve around work, school, and church.

When they got into the car after church that Sabbath, John exploded. "What does Pastor Matt mean about making friends with unchurched people? Why, everyone around here goes to church somewhere. They may not all be Adventists, but all our neighbors go to church. This is no mission field. Africa, India, China—now those are mission fields, but not here." Sue nodded in agreement, yet deep down she wondered whether Pastor Matt was right about their community.

After a scrumptious Sabbath lunch, John and Sue put a Bible DVD on the TV for the kids and went to the bedroom for their usual Sabbath afternoon nap. As they lay down, Sue brought up Pastor Matt's sermon again. "You know, John, I am not sure that all our neighbors are church-goers. Maybe more of them are unchurched than we realize. Wouldn't it be tragic if our neighbors were lost because we failed to witness to them?"

It was hard to nap that Sabbath afternoon, as they continued to reflect on Pastor Matt's sermon. Reflecting on the implications of neighbors that were lost, they began to focus on the attitudes of each of their neighbors toward religion, as well as their spiritual commitment and journey. They were in for a big surprise.

Next door was a Muslim family. They did not know their family name, but they thought the husband's name was Mohammad. They were certainly different. The wife dressed with a head covering, and the family rarely interacted with neighbors. In fact, John and his family were a little suspicious of them because of their Middle Eastern roots.

Across the street were Sally and Mike and their family. John and Sue chatted with these neighbors fairly often. They had a lot in common, since both couples had boys about the same age, and the children played together quite frequently. Religion had never been a topic of discussion between them. It seemed that this family never went to church, since they usually mowed the grass every Sunday morning. John had mentioned the Bible once in a conversation with Mike, who had responded by saying that he really did not believe in discussing religion.

The other next-door neighbors, Julie and Stan, were very involved in their jobs. In fact, Stan traveled a lot for his employer, and Julie worked long and late hours in the city. They both usually arrived home late at night. On weekends they had a tendency to party and had put on a few loud parties in the back yard on Saturday nights that evidently included a lot of drinking. John and Sue felt they had nothing in common with the lifestyle of Julie and Stan and had basically avoided them.

Other neighbors down the street, Joe and Mary, seemed like a nice couple. John and Sue had interacted with them a few times and had even invited them over for supper and games one night. Mary and Sue were somewhat friendly with each other and had gone shopping together a few times. Joe and John seemed to enjoy talking sports. Once the conversation had turned to religion, and Joe and Mary had indicated that they did not attend church, but they did consider themselves Christians. They felt that they worshiped God in their own way.

Then there was the house on the corner. John and Sue did not know what to think about this household that consisted of two men and a small boy around 6 years of age. They had warned their children not to go near the house or ever to enter the house, and they would not allow their boys to play with the boy who had two dads. This family definitely did not go to church anywhere, and their lifestyle scared John and Sue.

The other family on the cul-de-sac was a Hindu family from India. John and Sue really did not know them. The family kept mostly to themselves, but John and Sue had heard from the other families in the neighborhood that these neighbors were Hindus. This couple kept a nice-looking home and greeted John and Sue whenever they met, but other than that, there was not much communication between them.

Then there was Barbara, the neighborhood's resident atheist. She wanted nothing to do with religion and ridiculed anyone who did, including John and Sue. She had grown up in a conservative church with lots of rules and had finally "freed" herself from the restrictions of God. In college she had forsaken her religious roots and accepted an evolutionary explanation of life that left no room for God.

As John and Sue continued to think about each person in their neighborhood, they were shocked. Suddenly it dawned on them that they were the only ones in the neighborhood that even attended church! They pondered this for a while and remembered talking to a neighbor several blocks down who had indicated that they attended church fairly regularly. John and Sue could not remember which church they went to, but at least there was someone else who went to church nearby.

Could it be that their street was a mission field? Was Pastor Matt right after all? Was mainstream America as much a mission field as Africa and Saudi Arabia? The evidence was a bit overwhelming that afternoon—the fact was that 90 percent of the people in their neighborhood were unchurched. As they began piecing together the results of their discussion, they realized that not only were their neighbors unchurched, but their unchurched backgrounds were vastly different.

The backgrounds ranged from atheists, Hindus, and Muslims, to unchurched Christians, homosexuals, and those indifferent to religion. To their knowledge, only one other family who lived nearby actually went to church. John and Sue began to wonder if this was typical of the neighborhoods of other church members. Was their neighborhood odd? If other church members lived in similar neighborhoods, then maybe the pastor was right: they lived in a mission field. If this was true, it suddenly dawned on John and Sue that they must do something to spread the message of Jesus to their neighbors. But how? Each family was different. What approaches should they use?

## THE COMPLEXITY OF THE AMERICAN MISSION FIELD

To most American Adventists, the description you have just read may seem far-fetched. It is not. These are the new demographics. Go out into your neighborhood and do what John and Sue did. Discover how many people in your neighborhood actually go to church. You will be surprised to discover that the vast majority of people do not attend church regularly any longer. The people may indicate that they are Baptists, Catholics, or Methodists, but it does not mean that they go to church.

One Adventist pastor living in the Bible Belt—the southern United States—went out into his neighborhood and asked each family if they attended church regularly. He was surprised to discover that in his neighborhood, over 80 percent of the people did not attend church. And this was the Bible Belt. Welcome to twenty-first century America.

## UNCHURCHED AMERICANS

The neighborhood described at the beginning of this chapter is reflective of many American communities in the twenty-first century.

There is diversity in belief and lifestyle, exemplified by a community comprised of a variety of ethnicities and religions. Yet with all the diversity, few actually practice the faith they claim to embrace.

How many unchurched people are there in America? In the above scenario we hinted that it could be as high as 80 percent in the Bible Belt and obviously much higher elsewhere. In my studies I have discovered that the actual unchurched population is somewhere between 224 million and 251 million of the 300 million people in the United States. That means that somewhere around 50 million people attend church regularly. These figures are based on adding up the membership of all Christian churches, subtracting that figure from the general population, and then cutting the membership in half, based on the assumption that only half the membership of churches ever show up.

I believe this to be a conservative estimate. There are approximately 324,000 churches in the United States. The average attendance, according to George Barna, is around ninety people.[1] That would indicate a weekly attendance of around 29 or 30 million. Of course some people don't make it every week, but still attend somewhat regularly, so an active Christian membership of 50 million is possible.

Interestingly, 41 percent of Americans report that they went to church last week.[2] That would be 123 million people. Obviously, some got lost on their way there. Some people evidently feel that it is all right to lie about going to church. Even if all 123 million showed up, there would still be 177 million who did not. No matter how you look at, the vast majority of people in the United States today are no longer attending Christian churches.

In addition, many of those who do attend church are not even Christians.[3] They attend church regularly, but they know very little about the faith they claim to embrace. Many such people reside in the safe confines of the local Seventh-day Adventist Church. They attend, but they have no real, vital experience with Jesus Christ. To these people, the church has become a nice social club. They may have been raised in the church, and they appreciate the culture, but their religion does not translate into the vibrant relationship Jesus wants in His church.

## WHAT ARE THE UNCHURCHED LIKE?

There is no easy classification of the unchurched or non-Christians today. There is great diversity, as seen in John and Sue's neighborhood.

**1. The non-Christians.** Some that we would consider unchurched are not so much unchurched as non-Christian. This would include the Muslims, Hindus, Buddhists, etc. that reside in many major metropolitan areas of America. These people have their religion, but it is not Christianity. Some may wish to add to the non-Christian category those individuals who belong to the "heretical" sects of Christianity, such as Mormons and Jehovah Witnesses. These are churches that do not fully accept the divinity of Jesus and the authority of Scripture. The members of all these groups would be considered churched but wrongly churched. They certainly need evangelization.

**2. Nominal Christians.** A second unchurched group includes nominal Christians. They profess Christianity but rarely, if ever, attend. Many of the families in John and Sue's neighborhood would belong to this category. Many of them were brought up with a religious affiliation, but they don't practice it except for the rites of passage. If one were to ask people in this group whether they belonged to a church, they probably would answer yes and mention that they were Baptists, Methodists, Catholics, etc. They might not even hold membership, but that is how they were brought up, so they consider themselves to be a part of that particular religion.

**3. Those unhappy with the institutional church.** A third group of unchurched includes those who have become dissatisfied with the institutional church. They attend no church, preferring instead to worship God in their own way. They regard themselves as very spiritual and deeply committed to the Christian faith, but have been disillusioned by the trappings of the traditional church. Barna suggests that as much as 8 percent of the unchurched fit into this category.[4] Adventists have done a fairly good job of reaching into this group of unchurched. They respond positively to the public evangelistic approach used by most Adventist churches. They are the religiously unchurched.

**4. The post-moderns.** A fourth unchurched group contains what some call post-moderns. They do not believe in absolute truth. What is good for you is all right, but it might not be truth for me. Truth is relative. A growing group of Americans fit into this category. Most of them are not agnostic. They believe in God, but their God is a mixture of various ideologies to which they have been exposed. They have synchronized eastern and western religions and have created their own personal religion. These people will affirm you in what you believe, but it does not mean they are interested in following your truth.

**5. The atheists and agnostics.** A fifth group is made up of the unchurched who profess no faith. They do not believe in God—or they are agnostic. To them, faith has no part in their existence. They live life without any reference to God. In America, they represent a very small percentage of the population, but they are still part of the unchurched group.

**6. The gay community.** A sixth unchurched group is the homosexual community. They feel alienated from Christianity, especially conservative Christianity. Many of them were actually brought up in conservative Christian homes, but when the faith community rejected their lifestyle, they abandoned faith. A few have linked up with some of the liberal denominations that have embraced homosexuality as a viable lifestyle in harmony with Christian ideals. However, the vast majority of people in this community are turned off by conservative churches and view people who belong to them as prejudiced and mindless. This community presents a major challenge for conservative churches.

**7. The New-Age believers.** A seventh unchurched group includes those caught up in New Age ideology. Their religion is a mixture of paganism and Christianity, with no apologies offered for blending the two. Some in this group have even slipped into Satanic worship and witchcraft. The New Age group is one of the fastest-growing in America today. Their influence is being felt in places of power, such as Hollywood, where movies and television programming have been laced with New Age and spiritualistic influences. The result is that New Age beliefs and spiritualism have gone mainstream.

What is surprising is that many of the unchurched still have strong roots in Christianity. This is especially true in groups two and three. And both of these groups are large. It is these unchurched groups that Adventists traditionally have been able to penetrate. They are most open and susceptible to the messages of the three angels.

However, there are five other classifications of unchurched that we have identified. How are we going to reach them? The saving message of Jesus Christ must be introduced to all these groups, even the most difficult ones. Our traditional methods of evangelism will continue to work for groups two and three, but few people from the other groups will ever show up at a public evangelistic meeting. However, that does not mean that public evangelism will not influence them as part of a process of bringing them to Christ.

The Adventist church has a message for all people, including groups one, four, five, six and seven. We need to begin to formulate strategies and plans to reach all seven groups of unchurched. However, in this process we must not abandon what we are already doing well. We cannot afford to neglect groups two and three in the name of looking for souls in the other groups. Different churches will be able to concentrate on different groups. A conference should strategize to make certain that all groups in its territory are being reached. Too often we have divided our territory by geographic or ethnic boundaries and then focused on a church that would reach everyone in those boundaries. However, today we need to concentrate on planting churches that not only focus ethnically and geographically but also on one of the seven unchurched groups.

**8. Those who attend or belong to other Christian churches.** Another group that cannot be forgotten includes people that belong to and attend other Christian churches. Barna indicated that as many as 75 percent of the regular attendees in some denominations are not biblical Christians (this includes the Adventist church). These people certainly need to be reached with a more vibrant Christianity. And God also wants to share the unique Adventist message with many who are already vibrant Christians but whose faith will blossom with the addition of the Adventist message.

In the past, the vibrant Christian community provided most of the converts to Adventism. Our critics charged us with "sheep stealing." However, research has revealed that today Adventists are not doing a very good job in reaching other Christians. The Pentecostals and non-denominational churches take the lead in sheep stealing, while Adventists have lost the knack.[5]

Perhaps in reaction to our critics, we have stopped attempting to reach Christians of other faiths. If so, we need to improve in this area and begin once again unashamedly to call them into the full light of biblical truth. In reality, Regele's research indicated that Adventists are one of the best denominations in reaching the unchurched. For this we can praise God, but we must not neglect any group, for Adventists have been given a message for all people.

## POST-SECULARISM

While secularism continues to be the dominant feature of Europe and Australia, America has entered the post-secular age. That does not foretell a return to the church. The post-secular age is a religious age, but without the institutional church. That is probably the greatest change in the religious landscape of America in the twenty-first century. Writing at the end of the twentieth century, Thomas Bandy described the direction of secularism in the new century.

The biggest shock, however, is that on the brink of the twenty-first century, we are living in a post secular age! The admission of Harvey Cox in the preface of his recent book *Fire From Heaven* (Addison-Wesley, 1995) should strike the church like a bombshell. The author of the landmark 1965 book *The Secular City*, who influenced two generations of church leadership to reassess church life and mission in the face of the relentless march of secularity, writes twenty years later: "today it is secularity, not spirituality, that may be headed for extinction."[6]

One of the false assumptions made about today's unchurched is that they are secular. This is absolutely wrong. They are very spiritual, but not in the traditional way of Christianity. In fact, they may well be one of the most spiritual generations ever. This should suggest that God has opened up a door of spirituality that smart churches will use to break through to these people who are definitely seeking a spiritual connection.

Such people will not be interested by the presentation of objective truth, but instead, they will be won by discovering how that objective truth leads to a deeper experience with God. They are not interested in truth for the sake of truth but in truth that leads to a practical experience with God. They wish to reach out and touch Him. That is why the Pentecostals, with their heavy emphasis on experience, have been so successful. Adventists, on the other hand, have emphasized truth largely apart from experience. Both approaches are wrong. Perhaps Adventists could reposition themselves as the exponents of the truth that leads to the experience. Biblical religion blends both truth and experience—and so must Adventists.

## SUMMARY

The picture of mission in twenty-first century North America is not as clear as it was in the nineteenth or even twentieth centuries. We now live in a post-church society. Most people no longer attend church weekly. Many who don't attend are disenfranchised.  In this book we wish to examine how a church can reach out and touch these various populations with the everlasting gospel. We will discover some common denominators that churches will need to embrace, but from those common denominators will evolve different strategies for reaching the multi-faceted unchurched and churched populations that reside in modern North America.

## Notes:

1. Barna, George. September 2, 2003. "Small churches struggle to grow because of the people they attract." (http://www.barna.org/FlexPage. aspx?Page=BarnaUpdate&BarnaUpdateID=148).

2. Ibid.

3. Barna. January 29, 2002. "American faith is diverse, as shown among dive faith-based segments." (http://www.barna.org/FlexPage.aspx?Page=Barna Update&BarnaUpdateID=105).

4. Ibid

5. Regele, Mike. *Death of the Church* (Grand Rapids, MI: Zondervan, 1995), chapters 13 and 14.

6. Bandy, Thomas G. *Kicking Habits* (Nashville: Abingdon Press, 1997).

# CHAPTER TWO

# Creating the Culture of Evangelism

Most twenty-first century Adventist churches in North America face a daunting problem. In spite of the overwhelming evidence that North America is one of the greatest mission fields on the planet, most Adventist churches live their daily lives as if there were no crisis. Several have let the years slip by with no new people, except children of members, joining the church. In some churches baptisms are so rare that when two or three are baptized, the believers feel the latter rain has fallen.

I remember one church where I held an evangelistic series. At the end came several baptisms. When we attempted to fill the baptistry, we discovered it was the storage bin for the church. Not only that, the water had never even been hooked up. And the church was over twenty-five years old! Evidently there had been no baptisms in the church for nearly twenty-five years.

Sadly, what is considered normal for most North American Adventist churches is in fact living in direct disobedience to the Great Commission. Adventists claim to be the commandment-keeping people of God, but we have exempted the great commission from the commandments. Yet this is one of the greatest and most important commandments ordered by our Lord in His departing words to the disciples. We cannot and dare not be disobedient here. To fail in keeping this commandment is to stand in dereliction of duty. We must go forth and make disciples, or we are not a true Seventh-day Adventist church.

Most Adventist pastors are stymied by their church members' lack of interest in reaching the lost. The church seems to be more concerned with arguments over music and cheese than over reaching the lost. If half the energy that has been spent in the "worship wars" were spent on reaching the lost, we would be shocked at the results in most churches. It must be heart-wrenching for God to see churches fighting over miniscule issues, when so many people need to be reached with the authentic, everlasting gospel of Jesus Christ.

Yet it is not a hopeless situation. Research has revealed that there are many vibrant, growing Seventh-day Adventist churches in the twenty-first century. What is different about these churches? For the last few years in my church growth class at the seminary, I have assigned groups of students to select a conference in North America and choose the five churches in that conference with the highest rate of baptisms over the previous year. They have then called these churches and interviewed the pastor and/or lay leader to discover what was happening. We look at ten to fifteen conferences each year, which would represent fifty to seventy-five churches. Through the last three years, that represents 150 to 200 churches.

Many studies have been done on growing Adventist churches, but what some researchers have failed to do is distinguish between transfer growth and convert growth. You get different results when you exclude churches that are growing through transferred members. Many of these fast-growing Adventist churches are located in high Adventist population areas and are growing primarily because members are transferring from other Adventist churches. This is fine, but we must make certain that we don't copy these churches that are growing through transfers, and then expect convert growth as a result. It is critical to examine churches growing primarily by convert growth.

As I listened to and read the reports of the students who made the contacts, a few common denominators began to emerge. First of all, there is no magic pill that a church can swallow that will enable it to finish the work in its territory. Church growth is hard work, and church members must be committed to it. However, what I did notice about the churches growing by convert growth was that each of them had somehow created a culture of evangelism in their church.

In fact, it seemed to make little difference which methodologies the churches used, provided they had first of all created this culture of evangelism. Once the culture was in place, then almost any approach they used worked. Later on, we will examine some of the more common methodologies used by these growing Adventist churches. At this point, we must realize that it is not some new methodology that is important—it is the development of a culture of evangelism that is imperative. Once this happens, anything will work.

## WHAT IS A CULTURE OF EVANGELISM?

A culture of evangelism exists when reaching the lost permeates the entire fabric of the local church. This culture will occur when a church realizes that their self-identity is wrapped up in the fulfillment of the great commission. It is who they are. A church that has a culture of evangelism is clearly identifiable. When one talks to the members of such a church, they all resonate with the same urgency: their church exists to reach the lost. It is the burning passion that consumes them.

When a church has a culture of evangelism, evangelistic thinking reveals itself in every activity of the local church. It is not just the concern of the personal ministries committee or the evangelism committee. Reaching the lost is talked about on every committee and in every ministry of the church. Ministries exist to enable the church to fulfill the great commission. In a church with the culture of evangelism, the Pathfinder club, the Community Services group, and the Sabbath School will all be equally concerned that their ministry will enable the church to fulfill its mission.

In a church with the culture of evangelism, the monthly church board meeting will focus on reaching the lost. It will be the first item on the agenda, and most of the meeting time will be spent discussing how the church can be better equipped to fulfill the mission of Christ. Of course, this is what the *Church Manual* declares to be the main function of the church board, but a church with the culture of evangelism actually accomplishes it.

Not only does passion for the lost grasp the imagination of the institutional needs of the church, but it also captures the attention of the individual members. They live for the sake of reaching the lost. They may have a daily vocation, but it is the sideline in their life. They exist for the sake of reaching the lost. Their weekly paycheck enables them to support their family so that they can be involved in their real vocation—fulfilling God's mission. This is the all-consuming passion of their life.

What I am describing may sound hyperbolic to most readers. It certainly does not describe my church, you may be thinking. Yet it is the reality of the New Testament church. I realize I am describing the ideal, but the nearer we come to this ideal, the faster our church will grow. What the research reveals is that Adventist churches that have begun to grasp this culture are ones that are the growing in the twenty-first century. If there is a magic pill, this is it.

The reality is that most Adventist churches are nowhere near this ideal. This is why so few churches are growing. It is easy to blame the difficulties of evangelism on the materialism of North America and the Western world, but the reality is that the real problem is not in the external world that we cannot control, but with the internal passion of the church, which we can control. Yet it is far easier to blame the world, over which we have no power, than to ask ourselves what we can do to fulfill the mandate of the Master.

By now, some of you may be, figuratively at least, stomping your feet and saying: "True, true—but how can we create this kind of passion in our church?" And that is the real question we need to consider. Since most of our churches lack a culture of evangelism, and since that is the most basic ingredient for growth in our churches, then what can we do to create it?

## CREATING THE CULTURE

Pastor Matt in Chapter 1 had taken the first step, an approach most pastors use: he preached a sermon. This is always a good first step, although, as we will see, much more is needed. Notice also that Pastor Matt's sermon sprang from a passion for the lost that had begun to grip his own heart. This is where the process really begins: deep in the heart of the church leader.

Where does a pastor develop such a passion? Only from Jesus. This is why a lack of church growth is such a spiritual problem. One cannot spend significant time with the Master and not begin to feel His passion. See Him as the crucified Redeemer revealing such deep passion for the lost that He was willing to go to Calvary and pay the price of separation from God because the lost mattered so much to Him. One cannot truly spend time contemplating the ministry of Jesus without developing His passion for the lost. That is who Jesus is. He is the God who came seeking the lost. This was the driving passion of His life. Everything He did was for the sake of reaching the lost. Lost people matter to Jesus, and lost people are the center of His attention.

As the local church leader begins to develop this passion for the lost, it will soon be manifested in everything that happens in the church. Churches become reflections of their leaders. The passion of the leader will soon become the passion of the church. There can be no growing church without a leader who feels this passion for the lost.

This does not mean that if there is no growth in the church, the church has a leader without passion for the lost. This passion has to be in the leader first, but it must also translate to the members of the congregation. Through the years I have observed pastors with passion for the lost, but the church did not grasp their passion. This could be due to the pastor's inability to convey the passion, or it could be an outright rejection of the passion of Christ on the part of the church. However, growth will not take place unless this passion for the lost consumes the life of the church leader.

How then does the leader gain this passion? I have suggested spending time contemplating the life and death of Jesus. That is where it ultimately must begin. It is also important for leaders to pray for God to give them the passion of Christ for the lost. Prayer for this passion will bring the strong passion of Jesus to the heart of the church leaders, so they, like Jesus, will begin weeping over the lost in their community.

> If when they came together, they would not speak concerning the things to which they see objections, but would hold their mouth as with a bridle, and would seek the Lord in earnest prayer that His Holy Spirit might rest upon them, that they might have a burden for souls for whom Christ died, they would find that their darkness would flee away, and light and hope would come into their souls.[1]

When leaders pray for this passion, Jesus always answers. The leaders then become consumed with the need for reaching the lost. It will bother them that people are not being won to Christ in their territory. They will weep before God over the lost, crying to God for His power to create a breakthrough for God. Ellen White describes what this passion looks like:

> Why do not believers feel a deeper, more earnest concern for those who are out of Christ? Why do not two or three meet

together and plead with God for the salvation of some special one, and then for still another? In our churches let companies be formed for service. Let different ones unite in labor as fishers of men. Let them seek to gather souls from the corruption of the world into the saving purity of Christ's love.[2]

Let the workers grasp the promises of God, saying, "Thou hast promised, 'Ask, and ye shall receive.' I must have this soul converted to Jesus Christ." Solicit prayer for the souls for whom you labor; present them before the church as objects for the supplication. It will be just what the church needs, to have their minds called from their little, petty difficulties, to feel a great burden, a personal interest, for a soul that is ready to perish. Select another and still another soul, daily seeking guidance from God, laying everything before Him in earnest prayer, and working in divine wisdom. As you do this, you will see that God will give the Holy Spirit to convict, and the power of the truth to convert, the soul.[3]

Once the leader has partaken of the passion of Christ for the lost, it is time to preach to the congregation about the lost. Our preaching must stem out of our deep passion, placed in our hearts by the Christ who intensely seeks for the salvation of lost people. So it is not just preaching about the lost, but doing so as a reflection of the passion of Jesus for the lost.

Congregations will not immediately turn around after one sermon. It will take multiple sermons. Passion for the lost will come through in all the leader's sermons, not just when that is the specific topic. When the passion of Christ becomes our deep passion, we, like God, will not be able to control ourselves: we will have to actively go forth to reach the lost.

Congregants rarely remember a specific sermon. They remember illustrations, but not the details. Why then preach? What will be conveyed and ultimately adopted by the church will be the passion that they hear the preacher enunciating week after week. They may not remember the details, but they will begin to feel the passion.

One of the biggest barriers church leaders face in developing this culture of evangelism is a nagging doubt about some part of the Adventist message. Over the years I have observed pastors with doubts and have noticed that they rarely exhibited passion for reaching people. Why would you want to bring people into a church that you were not sure was 100 percent right? At times I have observed a pastor with such doubts, who finally got the doubts removed. Almost immediately a deep passion for the lost developed, and the pastor soon began bringing people into the church. There is a definite connection between belief in the Adventist message and a passion to reach people with God's last-day message.

God has called the Seventh-day Adventist Church into existence. It is God's remnant church. Exposing people to this last-day message is a life-or-death matter. The Adventist Church is not just another denomination; it is a movement called by God to prepare a people for the coming of Jesus. If this does not describe your feelings about the Adventist Church, then maybe you need to get your doubts settled so you can possess this passion.

## THE PASSION DISPLAYED

Now that you have imbibed the passion of Christ, and you have been expressing it in your sermons week by week, what else can you do to see the passion absorbed by the rest of the church? Sermons are basic and are probably the easiest part of the process, but this passion must then be woven into the entire fabric of the church. How does one communicate passion in the everyday life of the church?

Here are several practical suggestions. First, if the leader has passion for the lost, that leader will be actively seeking the lost. For example, if one preaches about reaching the lost but is not actively reaching out personally to bring lost people to Jesus, then the church will observe a contradiction between the life of the leader and the leader's words. When such disparity exists, the words spoken from the pulpit will fall on unhearing ears.

There must be consistency between what the pastor preaches and what the pastor lives. The life reveals how the passion is lived out. Members will catch what they see their leader doing. If the leader is bringing neighbors to church, the members will, too. If the leader is giving Bible studies, so will the members. Consistency here is absolute.

Second, tell stories that illustrate this passion for the lost. I am not talking about stories that are sermonic illustrations, but stories told throughout the church. They may be told in the missionary period before worship, or at social gatherings. Churches are always telling stories. Make certain your stories are consistent with passion for the lost. For example, back in the days when I pastored a church and had prayer meeting, I would always ask for prayer requests. I made certain that I also mentioned, without naming names, the people with whom I was studying. Telling members stories of people interested in the message always helps convey passion for the lost as the very basic ingredient of the church.

Third, the leader conveys this passion in all his personal contacts within the church. As the pastor visits with different families, the talk always moves to passion for the lost. Whether it is sharing the name of a lost acquaintance who needs prayer, or some other avenue, the leader never allows a visit to conclude unless some time is spent communicating the passion.

As this passion for the lost begins to spread beyond the church pastor to many of the lay leaders in the church, their collective passion will then have an impact on what is happening in the local church. For example, when nominating committee time rolls around, people are selected for church office because they are demonstrating in their lives the passion of God for the lost. The church will not put people into major positions of leadership who are not living this Great Commission mandate. Obviously, this cannot be done until the culture of evangelism has begun to consume the church leadership.

Sadly, many churches select leaders on the basis of money, power, and influence. What is suggested here is a total abandonment of that approach and an acceptance of the passion of God as the determining factor. In other words, if you had two equally qualified leaders, you would choose the one with the greatest passion for the lost. This, of course, cannot be legislated, but is something that will occur as the passion of God consumes the church.

Consistency in all aspects of the church is the next necessity as the church takes passion for the lost as its focus. The local church budget will now reflect the priority of God for the lost. It will now assign funds in a way that reflects this priority. The church will not be consumed with just maintaining a building but will instead become passionate about how that building can be used to assist Jesus in reaching the lost.

## THE RESULTS

Can you imagine a church like this? You may think this is a pipe-dream that could never be fulfilled, but the reality is that some Adventist churches are beginning to look like this, and some of them are experiencing amazing growth. In developing countries, the Adventist Church is experiencing a 10 percent to 20 percent annual growth rate, but at least one large Adventist church in North America is experiencing more than a 20 percent annual conversion growth rate. The abundant growth rate of the Third World can happen in North America, but the heart of the church must beat with the passion of God.

All growing churches are not initially consumed with the passion of God. Growth occurs as soon as a church begins to move into the culture of evangelism. Spectacular growth takes place when that passion becomes the all-absorbing life of the church.

The more I study church growth, the more I am convinced that what we have discussed in this chapter is the heart of the issue. We can put on the trimmings and create growth for a short period, but unless the passion of God is there, the growth will be sporadic and short lived. I am convinced that rather than recommend "methodologies," we need to help our churches develop this passion for the lost. Once it is in place, any methodology will work. This is the bottom line. Success or failure in church growth begins and ends here.

Church growth authorities in the past have referred to this as a "church growth conscience." And that is exactly what it is. What is a conscience? A conscience is a feeling deep inside that tells me what is right or wrong. We are not born with a good conscience. Our conscience needs to be educated. When it is educated, then we feel guilty when we do something wrong. This is not a false guilt, but a genuine God-given guilt.

Before I was an Adventist, during my teenage years, my two favorite foods were pork chops and fried clams. I could never get enough of them. My conscience never bothered me when I consumed them with relish. Now if I would even touch one of these foods, it would bother me. Why? My conscience has been educated, and if I would eat such an unhealthy item today, the guilt would be enormous.

Our North American churches need to have their consciences educated on the passion of God. When that happens, it will bother them when the church is not growing. If no one was baptized last month, the subject will come up at the church board, and the board members will hold themselves accountable. When the culture of evangelism is in place, it will bother the church leadership when growth is not happening, because they know the church exists for the purpose of fulfilling the passion of God for the lost.

A theology of outreach and proclamation must be deeply rooted in the very psyche of the church. This is who we are. Our self-identity as a church is all wrought up with this insatiable passion of God for the lost. We cannot contain ourselves. We have to seek the lost, because that is who God is, and we are His people and are reflective of His character and His passion.

As a result, the church will be willing to pay whatever price is needed to bring about growth. The church recognizes that it is not a social club that exists for the benefit of the members but a mission agency involved in the work of the Redeemer-God. There is, therefore, no cost too great for the church to pay. Everything the church does revolves around the process of reaching the lost. The members take this as their self-identity; they are indeed consumed with the passion of God for the lost.

Isn't it time now to begin to ask God to instill this passion in your own heart, as well as in the heart of the church? If Adventists truly believe that God has called this church into being to give the final message to the inhabitants of Planet Earth, then we have no choice. Our self-identity as a church is totally absorbed with the fulfillment of the three angels' messages. We have no choice. If we are the people of God in earth's last hour, then we must be consumed with the passion of God. We must become a mission-centered church. The culture of evangelism must permeate every fiber of our being—or we are not God's final remnant.

## Notes:

1.  White, Ellen G. *Fundamentals of Christian Education* (Nashville, TN: Southern Publishing Association, 1923), 207.

2.  White, Ellen G. Testimonies for the Church, vol. 7 (Mountain View, CA: Pacific Press Publishing Association, 1948), 21.

3.  White, Ellen G. *Medical Ministry* (Mountain View, CA: Pacific Press Publishing Association, 1963), 244, 245.

# CHAPTER THREE

# Common Methods Growing Churches Use

Once a culture of evangelism has been established in the church and the passion of God for the lost is the consuming fire of its believers, then almost any evangelistic method will work. The growing churches we have studied have few things in common. They use different methodologies—yet they all work. The only conclusion we can draw is that it is not the methodology that works—it is the consuming passion of the church that contributes to the success of the church in convert growth.

But there are some common elements that seem to exist in most growing churches. The two most prominent methods we have discovered are the ability of the church to galvanize the laity into ministry for the lost—and the use of public evangelism. Yet non-growing churches will also utilize these methodologies without producing significant growth. What is the difference? The growing churches have utilized these methodologies *along with* the culture of evangelism.

## UTILIZATION OF LAITY

Many churches have created lay ministry programs, but still do not produce outstanding convert growth. However, the churches that are reaching lost people have not only reawakened the laity to their responsibility, but they have been able to translate that awakening into actual work for the salvation of lost people. In some of the growing churches we have found up to 80 percent of the laity involved in some kind of ministry.

Here is what I believe is happening. The culture of evangelism operating in the church results in members having a greater desire to share their faith and to be involved. In other words, you can't force members to get involved in ministry through guilt. However, when passion for reaching the lost is present, members want to be involved, and they want to get trained for their ministry.

I have observed many pastors through the years who get excited about lay ministry after reading some of my books, such as *Revolution in the Church*.[1] They have then called their members to a training event, but very few ever show up, and the pastor becomes discouraged. Here is the problem. The culture of evangelism must first be established. Once this passion for the lost becomes the mind-set of the church, the members will ask to be trained so that they can get involved. In our desire to quickly move the church ahead, we sometimes bypass the important step of creating the culture. If you do so, you will not succeed. Lay involvement must spring out of a renewed understanding and commitment to the mission of the church.

Dr. Kenneth Van Wyk several years ago observed the relationship between the culture of evangelism (mission mentality) and lay involvement:

> The church is a training center where the people of God are equipped for their respective areas of ministry and mission. Nurture, indeed, comes as a by-product of being equipped and involved in ministry. My experience in Christian education is that a mission mentality in the church motivates people to training and produces astounding results in personal spiritual growth as well as church growth.[2]

As laity are dispatched into ministry, it is important that there be balance in their assignments. You don't want all of them on the front lines. You need the "backup troops." A good ratio would be that one out of every five people involved in the church be involved in outreach. In other words, if you had 100 laity involved in ministry, twenty of them would be involved in outreach ministry and the other eighty involved in assimilating the new members and keeping the machinery of the church in good operation.

We are not interested in just getting numbers on the church books—

we are interested in souls prepared for the coming of Jesus. This is why it is so crucial to have a balance in the dispatching of the workers in the local church. Keeping people in the church is just as important as getting them in the first place. However, the reality is that most churches are spending little time in outreach and most of their time in nurture. So the present problem is the opposite. We are not currently in danger of too much emphasis on outreach. Our problem, in reality, is getting the 20 percent involved in outreach.

The basic issue to recognize is that once the church has grasped the culture of evangelism, it appears that one of the first things that then needs to happen is the employment of the laity in ministry. To attempt to put people into ministry without the culture in place will result in the placement of members in the wrong kinds of ministry. It is not just placing people in ministry in harmony with their spiritual gifts but maintaining balance between nurture and outreach. A church could conceivably have 100 percent of its members involved in ministry and still not grow. This would occur if all members were dispatched to nurture ministries. The balance is crucial for success.

## PUBLIC EVANGELISM

As church growth students have researched churches with the most baptisms, inevitably they will come back and state that there is nothing in common among them. In fact, some have said the only thing in common was that they held a meeting. And that is true. Public evangelism is still playing a vital role in Adventist church growth.

This is not true in evangelical Christianity generally, but it is a clear difference in Adventism. This is why Adventist churches cannot completely copy the methodologies of the evangelicals. The techniques do not produce the same results in Adventism. It appears that there has to be some format for teaching the Adventist message. And the best format we have discovered is public evangelism. Public evangelism can be done in various forms. All churches are not using the same formula. Some use the traditional five-week, prophecy-oriented preaching series, while others use a seminar approach or a Sabbath morning covering of the message. The main point is that they share the unique Adventist message publicly in some way.

This finding would differ with other studies that have been done of Adventist church growth. However, most of those studies have not differentiated between transfer growth and convert growth. If you combine them, you end up with different results. In those studies, it has been shown that public evangelism does not play a significant role in church growth. One needs to understand, however, what is being measured. If you include churches growing primarily by transfer growth, they will overshadow the churches growing by convert growth, since most Adventist growing churches are growing by transfer growth.

When one separates out the churches primarily growing by convert growth, then public evangelism becomes a major player in church growth. I have personally examined many of the churches that have been using a contemporary approach to worship so that they can reach the unchurched. At least this is their intention. However, when I examine their baptismal record, I discover very few adult baptisms. Yet the church is growing. How? It is primarily by transfer growth.

Most of the successful contemporary churches I have observed have been birthed in an area where there are large Adventist settlements or institutions. Their freshness and contemporary style has attracted many former and inactive Adventists, as well as some of the disenfranchised people attending other churches. At first these churches grow rapidly, but then they have a tendency to level off and decline. One cannot build a church on the disenfranchised, or it will ultimately self-destruct. It is amazing how many of these churches Adventist leaders flocked to observe a few years ago, that no longer exist or have even left the denomination.

These kinds of churches do have a place, especially if they can reach out to former and inactive members and get them involved. However, if they don't couple that effort with the reaching of new people, these churches usually do not continue for long. The tragedy has been that others have attempted to copy this contemporary model and assumed they could have similar success in their community. However, most communities do not have a lot of former Adventists living there, and the model does not work. The only real result is that this model makes existing Adventists angry over the style of worship. One must understand that the reason for the success of these churches is that they are planted where there are already a lot of Adventists that can be enticed to join the new church.

With evangelicals, the seeker service is built on the premise that when people decide to go to church, they will show up on a Sunday morning. Therefore the Sunday morning service is geared for their reception. Obviously, that does not translate into Adventism. Most people don't just decide to go to a church on a Sabbath morning, except in high-density Adventist areas. In those communities the seeker service will work for us, but it does not seem to work apart from the Adventist community, unless something else is added to the mix.

In contrast, a few Adventist churches utilize a contemporary approach to worship but are also successful in reaching the unchurched. They are baptizing significant numbers of people and are some of the best-growing churches in Adventism. They are also faithful to our Adventist heritage and doctrine and do not compromise the faith in order to reach people. So the issue is not whether one uses contemporary worship. Some churches that reach new people and some that reach only former Adventists are using contemporary worship.

What is the difference? The churches that are reaching new people also have public evangelism somewhere in their programs. This is the amazing difference between those churches that reach new people and those that are reaching the inactives. I believe that if the churches reaching the inactives would add public evangelism into their programming, they could reach the unchurched also in their community. From my experience and observation of over forty years, as well as studies we have done, it has become abundantly clear that public evangelism must be a vital part of the prescription for successful convert growth in Adventism.

This does not mean that everyone must hold a five-week meeting. There are many ways that public evangelism can be done. What we are suggesting here is that in some way the church needs to expose people to the unique Adventist message and publicly invite them to become members. In all honesty I must say that I have seen a few churches experiencing convert growth without public evangelism, but they have been extremely rare. This is why I strongly suggest that any church serious about reaching the lost include some form of public evangelism in its growth mix.

## GROWTH MIX

What do we mean by "growth mix"? A growth mix includes the various forms and methods of evangelism a church uses to reach people for Jesus. What I am strongly suggesting here is that public evangelism, in most cases, must be part of that mix for successful Adventist church growth. Growing Adventist churches have put together a successful growth mix that fits their congregations and their style of ministry.

A growth mix makes certain that the church is doing sowing, cultivating, and reaping. This is another factor that appears to be common among Adventist churches growing through convert growth. They have planned a process of evangelism that involves all three natural steps.

Evangelism is not an event—it is a process. Growing churches have learned this. Many Adventist churches will experience periodic growth when they hold an evangelistic meeting. But unfortunately, to them, evangelism is an event. When it is over, they can go back to life as usual. The difference between these churches and those that experience continuing growth is that this latter group of churches views evangelism as a process, of which public evangelism is only one part—the reaping part.

Steadily growing churches have realized that there is more to evangelism than the public meeting. One cannot continually reap if one has not continually sown. What we have noticed in the studies we have done is that a meeting is rarely successful if there has not been a clearly thought-out strategy to prepare the community for the meetings. The harvest reaped is compatible with and proportionate to the seed sown and cultivated.

Yet in these steadily growing churches this process is not confined to just one evangelistic meeting. Some churches will enter into a process of sowing, cultivating, and reaping for one meeting—and then it stops. With the growing churches this is a continuous action. As soon as people are reaped, the process repeats. The latest people won are immediately put to work for their friends and family, preparing them for the next reaping event. The entire church is constantly involved in sowing, cultivating and reaping. The process of evangelism is a vital part of the life of the entire church.

Few people are won to Christ through one exposure. They need multiple exposures to the gospel. This is why it is imperative that a church not put all its eggs in one basket. They need multiple approaches for the many and varied minds that exist in their community. Process evangelism is best illustration by the following diagram:

| 1 | 2 | 3 | 4 | 5 | 6 | 7 | 8 | 9 | 10 |
|---|---|---|---|---|---|---|---|---|----|

On a scale of 1 to 10, the 1 represents a person who is extremely negative about the Seventh-day Adventist Church. He is the one who sees the sign on the church, spits, and walks on the other side of the street. In contrast, the 10 represents a person ready to jump right into the baptistry. Everyone is somewhere on this scale in their relationship to the church.

The people who normally attend an Adventist evangelistic meeting are 8, 9, or 10 on the scale. They are ready to be reaped. They have been prepared by God or through church members, used by God. They make a decision in the evangelistic meeting and are quickly baptized into the Adventist Church. If a person who is a 3 happens to come to the evangelistic meeting, they normally would not return. It wasn't for them. This is understandable when one realizes they are a 3 on the scale. They probably should never have been invited to the meeting. They were not ready for reaping. Remember, public evangelism is the reaping part of the process. The 3s and 4s need cultivation before exposing them to a reaping event.

Mary is a 3 on the scale. She has just recently gone through a divorce. An Adventist friend invites her to attend a divorce recovery seminar offered by the church. She attends and is extremely grateful to the church for the help provided. Is she now ready to be invited to the evangelistic meeting and reaped? No. She has moved up the receptivity scale, and while formerly a 3, she may now be a 5. It will usually take several exposures for a person to move up to the 8, 9, or 10 level, where they should be invited to the reaping event.

Most people are between 1 and 7 on the scale. If the church does nothing to move these people up the scale in their receptivity but continues to hold meetings aimed at the 8s, 9s, and 10s, pretty soon the pool of people in the 8, 9, and 10 categories will dry up, and the public meeting will not be successful. This is why it is so critical for the church to possess a process understanding of growth. If the church is continually ministering to people in the 1 through 7 area, there will be a constant supply of people moving into the reaping range.

Sometimes churches get so excited about meeting the needs of the people in the 1 through 7 range that they spend all their time seeking to minister to them and never hold a reaping event. These churches do not grow. Once you neglect any part of the process, growth will stop. Growth is a process, and if you neglect this concept, you cannot expect to see new people continually joining the church.

The growth mix found in differing churches will vary. One size does not fit all. Each church will need to discover which events are parts of their own process. The important thing to remember is that all three parts of the process are in continual operation. In other words, keep monitoring what your church should be doing in the areas of sowing, cultivating, and reaping. Neglect any part of this process, and growth will not happen.

## CONCLUSION

In this chapter we have observed two methodologies that seem to be common to growing Adventist churches. These churches have established the culture of evangelism where the laity are utilized in meaningful ministry, and second, they have a process of evangelism in operation that includes sowing, cultivating, and reaping events. Most of them are utilizing public evangelism in some form as their reaping event.

This process of evangelism permeates the thinking of these growing churches on every level. When process thinking controls the church, the members realize that every ministry of the church is involved in soul winning. Thus the Sabbath School, the church school, the Pathfinder club, and the Dorcas Society are all making a contribution to the process of winning people to Jesus. This is not just theory—it becomes a living reality for these churches.

## Notes:

1. Burrill, Russell. *Revolution in the Church* (Fallbrook, CA: Hart Research Center, 1993).

2. Van Wyk, Kenneth. *Pastor's Church Growth Handbook*, vol. 1, edited by Win Arn (Pasadena, CA: Church Growth Press, 1979), 134.

# CHAPTER FOUR

# A Brief Review of Church Growth Theory

Donald McGavran, founder of the church growth movement, enunciated seven major components of church growth theory. These seven factors must be in place for a church to grow, and they are still valid today. What are they?[1]

1. A pastor who is a possibility thinker and whose dynamic leadership has been used to catalyze the entire church into action for growth. Early church growth scholars quickly recognized the critical role pastors play in church growth. They correctly observed that the growth history of the church kept changing as pastors changed. A church could be growing, a new pastor would arrive, and it would stop growing—or vice versa. The leadership of the pastor and his ability to see the possibilities for growth and then create the vision to move into the future is absolutely critical for growth to occur. The key issue is the creation of the mission mentality or evangelism culture. It takes strong pastoral leadership for that to happen.

2. A well-mobilized laity which has discovered, developed, and is using all their spiritual gifts for growth. This major component we have commented on extensively in the previous chapter. The pastor cannot be a lone ranger. He or she must be able to mobilize the laity behind the vision and enable God's people to utilize all the spiritual gifts that He has placed in the church.

3.  A church large enough to provide the range of services that meets the needs and expectations of its members. Church growth scholars did not mean that only megachurches could be adequate in this area. In fact, during the 70s, when these components were discovered, megachurches hardly existed. McGavran simply recognized that a church needs to be large enough to accomplish what it feels God has called it to do. That could be a fifty-member church as well as a 1,000-member church.

4.  The proper structural balance of the dynamic relationship between celebration, congregation, and cell. "Celebration" as used by these early church growth scholars was not about "celebration" churches such as those that have developed in Adventism. They used the word *celebration* to indicate that the church member needs to feel they are part of something bigger. Adventists usually accomplish this at camp meetings or General Conference sessions. Some larger churches also can give this impression to believers. "Congregation" referred to a group of around fifty people that each member becomes acquainted with in the church. The member might know their names, but has not formed a deep relationship with these people. "Cell" is a reference to a small, intimate group of ten to twelve people, in which the members share their life in Christ and build deep relationships. To be healthy, a church needs to provide all three exposures. Adventists have done fairly well with congregation and celebration. Our weakest area has been in the realm of the cell or small group. As a result, many Adventists are only loosely attached to their church and do not have solid relationships in the body.

5.  A membership drawn basically from one homogeneous unit. This component became the most controversial principle of church growth theory. McGavran was descriptive here and not prescriptive. His studies revealed that most congregations ended up reaching people who were like them. As a result, large segments of the harvest were unreaped. That is why it was so necessary to plant new homogeneous churches in these unreached people groups.

6.  The use of evangelistic methods that have proven to work and focus on making disciples. McGavran was concerned that churches had a tendency to keep doing the same thing year after year, even though the results were not good. To him it made sense that a

church should evaluate what it was doing against the backdrop of the Great Commission. Were the methods successful? Churches should not use evangelistic tools just because they have always done it that way.

Interestingly, an Adventist church could hold evangelistic meetings year after year with little or no results and could easily conclude that the methodology no longer works. Yet, as seen in the previous chapter, the methodology is clearly working in hundreds of Adventist churches. So what is the problem? It might be that the church has conducted meetings as an *event* rather than as part of the evangelistic *process,* or perhaps they are holding meetings in place of establishing a culture of evangelism in the church. It would be easy to conclude that they should cease to hold evangelistic meetings, convinced they no longer work, when the problem is not in the meetings but in the lack of a holistic approach to evangelism. This is why a clear, well-thought-out evaluation of what is happening is so important. A church cannot simply look at surface methodology but must also examine why that methodology is no longer working.

7.  A philosophy of ministry that has its priorities arranged in biblical order. According to McGavran, biblical order occurred when the salvation of the lost took top priority in the church. Either the Great Commission is the main concern of the church—or we are following religious philosophy rather than the Savior. By mandating the Great Commission, Jesus established the making of disciples as the chief work of the church. Any church that puts anything else over the making of disciples has its priorities arranged in a non-biblical order.[2]

## AXIOMS OF CHURCH GROWTH[3]

In addition to the major components of church growth theory, the early scholars of church growth identified four axioms they found to be true in pursuing the fulfillment of the Great Commission in local churches.

1.  The pastor must want the church to grow and be willing to pay the price. Once again, church growth is seen as being dependent on the pastor and his or her willingness to pay the price of growth. That price includes very hard work. Growth-oriented pastors consistently work longer hours. But it is not just working

longer but working smarter. These pastors galvanize their whole membership for the accomplishment of the Great Commission. Many pastors are not strongly motivated to get more members. They have all they can do just to pastor the ones they already have. So part of the cost of growth is that the pastor must be willing to have members he/she cannot pastor. The pastor must be willing, therefore, to train elders and other members to do the work of pastoral care.

2.  The members must want the church to grow and be willing to pay the price. Not only must the pastor be committed to growth, but so must the congregation. We have already noticed this axiom in the previous chapters. Sometimes the pastor is willing to pay the price for growth, but the members are not. The price members pay is that they may not know everyone in the church anymore; in addition, they might lose some of their positions. Then there is the problem of overcrowding and the need to plant a new church or build a bigger one. Are the members committed to paying the price of growth?

    In one church that I pastored many years ago, we were growing rapidly, with nearly 100 baptisms a year. One of my elders came to me to express his concern. He said: "Pastor, we have a problem in our church." Of course I was anxious to hear about the problem. He went on to explain that we had too many new members! That may sound shocking, for this is what the church is all about, but I needed to hear him out. In the past, he had always known everyone in the church. Now there were many people in church on Sabbath whom he did not know. Furthermore, he was concerned that the old members would lose control of the church. These are legitimate concerns that have to be addressed. Fortunately, I was able to help him see that this was a positive thing, but many times church leaders are not willing to pay the price, and they will sabotage growth.

3.  The church must agree that the goal of evangelism is to make disciples. McGavran defined *disciple* as the "initial bringing to Christ." Thus the axiom was meant to convey that evangelism should major in bringing people to Christ and not in developing them into mature Christians. While I would agree with McGavran's intent, I would not want to limit discipleship to just the initial coming to Christ. Our goal is not just to get people in

the door but to help them become fully devoted disciples of Jesus Christ, ready to meet Jesus when He comes.[4]

4. The church must not be suffering from a terminal illness. Obviously, churches afflicted with a terminal illness are unable to fulfill the Great Commission.[5]

## Terminal Illnesses[6]

McGavran defined eight illnesses afflicting churches that he considered terminal. He then proceeded to assign them names that sound like diseases. In the author's opinion, some of these are not as hopeless as others. However, it is true that if they are not addressed, they will result in the demise of the church.

## 1. Ethnikitis, or Ghost Town Disease

This disease-sounding affliction is a problem in all kinds of churches. It has afflicted many Adventist churches as well. Take, for example, the First Seventh-day Adventist Church in a downtown metropolis. For years it has been the flagship church in that area. It was the plum church for a pastoral assignment. To be the pastor there was to have prestige. However, over the last several years this church has been declining. All attempts to turn it around have failed.

Here is the problem. When First Church began, the neighborhood around the church was primarily peopled by middle-class whites. Now, fifty years later, the neighborhood around the church is populated largely by low-income Hispanics. As Hispanics moved into the area, the whites slowly moved out to the suburbs. New churches were launched in suburbia, and the membership of First Church began to decline. Out of loyalty, a few members continued to drive to First Church each Sabbath, but then quickly retreated to their suburb for the rest of the week. They showed no interest in the community around the church. When members would attempt to bring their friends from the suburbs to church, the friends indicated it was too far to travel. They preferred a church closer to home. As the children of these members grew up, they did not have the loyalty to First Church, so they began attending the churches in suburbia.

The result of this scenario is a church populated by one kind of people, and surrounded by another kind of people—and the two never interact. Unless First Church can find a way to minister to the surrounding Hispanic community, with the idea of turning the church over to them, then ultimately, either First Church will sell the building and move to the suburbs, or it will finally conclude that its ministry is over and shut the doors. There is no hope to revive such a church without these changes. This is why Ethnikitis is a serious, terminal illness, affecting primarily urban churches. All such churches will eventually die unless they turn their church over to the new ethnic group.

## 2. Old Age

While Ethnikitis is a disease primarily affecting urban churches, old age is a similar disease facing rural churches. Many Adventist churches began in rural America. In fact, Adventism in North America has been primarily a rural movement. Many small towns and communities had an Adventist church. However, migration to the cities has drained many of these churches of their membership. It is not only the church in rural America that is dying, the towns themselves are dying. Sometimes the only building left in town is the church. Many of these churches continue to struggle year after year. The worshipers can easily be counted on one's fingers. The members are old, and it is obvious that death for these churches is just around the corner.

Since people are migrating out of these towns, and few people are moving in, the prospect of new members is rapidly diminishing. It will not be long before such churches will close. Is there hope for such churches? I wish there were, but McGavran identified this as a terminal illness, and the last forty years have demonstrated that he is correct. Unless new people begin moving into the community, such a church cannot grow, and therefore it will die.

## 3. People Blindness

This disease is more easily corrected than the previous two maladies. This is the failure of the church to observe the many cultural differences of people that surround the church. They assume that most everyone in the community is like them and that if they reach these people, they are reaching the community. However, no American community in the twenty-first century is monolithic. Numerous people groups exist, even in the same cultural or ethnic pool.

When a church fails to reach out to other groups in their area and makes no provision to expand beyond the homogeneous group that exists in the church, then McGavran suggests the church will ultimately die. Churches live and die in one homogenous unit. In order to grow, a church must continually be reaching out to new homogeneous units of people. So this disease has a remedy. The church can become aware of the different people in its community and reach out to them with methodologies that connect with these new groups.

Reaching new cultural groups can cause severe problems for the church if the members insist that their cultural expression of faith is the only way things can be done. Reaching new groups means sharing different cultural expressions, especially in the area of worship. If a church cannot do that, it will die.

### 4. Hyper-Cooperativism

This is a malady that is more apt to afflict non-Seventh-day Adventist churches than it is Adventist ones, but it can still occur, so we should look at it. McGavran observed that churches that only did evangelism when there was a joint evangelistic event, in which all denominations participated, did not grow. The local church had to be central in the evangelistic process.

Likewise, if the only evangelistic meeting an Adventist church engages in is the one where all the Adventist churches in town come together to sponsor a meeting, little permanent growth will occur in the church. This does not mean the church should not engage in large city-wide meetings, with all the churches coming together. The point here is that this should not be the only evangelism done.

I was pastoring a church in an urban area. The conference had invited a very prominent evangelist to hold a series of meetings in one of the large auditoriums in the city that seated 3,000 people. All the churches were to participate, but no one church owned the meetings. There was no attempt to create ownership among the churches. The result was that on opening night, only 400 people attended. The Adventist population in the city was over 2,000. Soon the meetings dwindled to around 200 each night in an auditorium seating 3,000. Few positive results occurred. If the participating churches had decided that public evangelism did not work because of their experience with that meeting, and therefore this was the only time they did evangelism, then those churches would eventually die. However, in my church, six months later we held a meeting with just my church participating, and we baptized fifty people.

This malady is easy to eliminate. Each local church must develop its own strategy of evangelism. While they may at times join forces with other local churches, they will regularly conduct their own local meetings. Only then can the church grow.

## 5. Koinonitis

This disease is drawn from the Greek word, *koinonia,* meaning fellowship. When this disease afflicts the church, the focus is all on internal relationships within the church. In a certain sense the church has become a social club where the members enjoy each other's company, but there is no concern to reach out to new people and bring them to Jesus. This disease is very prominent in many Adventist churches.

Those who grow up in an Adventist culture assume knowledge of the culture. They fail to realize that new people joining the church discover quickly that they have entered into a foreign culture. If those already in the church do not extend the hand to help these new people adapt to the cultural changes, the new ones will quickly be migrating out the back door. A church having problems assimilating new members may be afflicted with this serious disease.

The evangelistic meetings in one church ended on a Saturday night with a spectacular baptism of over thirty new people into the local Adventist church. For five weeks the members had come out night after night, supporting the meetings. They rejoiced over these precious new people who had accepted the message, but they were exhausted and ready to get back to normal. So next Sabbath when the new people came to church, it looked much different. There were no greeters in the parking lot. When the new ones entered the foyer, a greeter quickly handed them a bulletin. They struggled to find the correct Sabbath School class. They had been used to vibrant lessons and inspiring music and sermons in church. But on this Sabbath a man got up and read an article for the sermon. What had happened? They figured they were in the wrong church, so they didn't come back.

It would be easy to conclude that this problem developed because the evangelist had not taught the church members sufficiently. Or could it have happened because the members failed to reach out and embrace the new ones, drawing them into the church by helping with the adjustment to the culture of that local church? So often we "dip them and leave them." Once they are baptized, the new members have to fend for themselves. Sadly, few survive.

This disease, while problematic, does have solutions and remedies. The church needs to move out of its comfort zone, embrace the new people, and help them feel at home. This church needs to help the beginners feel the wonderful koinonia that does exist in the church. Only if it can assimilate the newcomers can a church truly be a growing church.

## 6. SOCIOLOGICAL STRANGULATION

This sounds like a very serious disease, and it is. It recognizes that the ability of the church to grow is limited by the space available for new people. Whenever a church reaches 80 percent of its seating capacity, its parking space, or its Sabbath School facilities, it will stop growing.

I was pastor of a large church with 500 members on the books. For the previous ten years before my arrival, the membership had fluctuated between 500 and 525. The sanctuary seated 325 people, but the Sabbath attendance was only 280. I recognized that they were at the 80 percent factor and that it was hindering their growth. Available space alone does not guarantee growth, but lack of space definitely hinders growth. There simply is no place to put new people. North Americans like to have space. Just look at any airport waiting area. There are plenty of seats available, but people will stand rather than sit close to a stranger.

Recognizing the problem, I brought it to the church board and offered three solutions. They could plant a new church, build a new church, or go to two services. The board responded with a fourth suggestion: none of the above. In my youthful enthusiasm I declared that this was not an option and pushed them to go to two services. In hindsight, I should have allowed some time for them to think it over and get used to the idea, for during the entire five years of my pastorate there, they resented the second service.

Yet, you cannot argue with the success. Quickly, our attendance shot up until we had reached between 450 and 500 attending, where we plateaued, because once again, second service was filled up. When I left the congregation, they planted a new church, with fifty people going to the new site. They then suggested that they no longer needed the second service, even though they had an attendance of 400 and a sanctuary that was crowded to capacity at 325. Soon the attendance dwindled back to 280 and, at times, even descended to as low as • 150. The 80 percent factor is real.

When I arrived at my next church, I discovered a church with a seating capacity of 500, but again, an attendance of 280. This time the sanctuary space was not hindering growth—it was the Sabbath School space for the children's divisions. The church decided to build an addition to the church to accommodate the need. To do so meant they had to utilize part of the parking lot for the new building. In anticipation, we first added an additional parking lot to replace what we were about to lose. Amazingly, our attendance shot up by fifty people each Sabbath with the additional off-street parking. When we broke ground for the new addition and lost the parking space, the attendance dropped by fifty people. It is amazing how accurate the 80 percent factor is in Adventist churches. In inner city churches the parking space issue does not hold, because there is no expectation that there will be parking space for everyone. Also, some ethnic groups will tolerate sitting closer together, so the ratio may rise to 90 percent of the seating capacity in those churches.

A church, however, should not wait until it hits the 80 percent factor before doing something about the available space. Otherwise, the growth curve will be broken, and the church will lose momentum. Once growth momentum is lost, it is very difficult to regain. Therefore, a church should anticipate that in one year they will have reached the 80 percent factor and make plans to do something about it as they approach the maximum ratio. This way, they can keep their growth moving forward. There are three solutions to the 80 percent factor: build a new church, plant a church, or go to multiple services. The choice belongs to the church, but it must make one of these choices or risk being unfaithful to the Great Commission.

## 7. ARRESTED SPIRITUAL DEVELOPMENT

This is a disease that primarily affects new Adventists. There is rapid spiritual development occurring with these people during most evangelistic meetings. However, after they are baptized there is no more spiritual growth. It is as if they have now arrived and there are no more heights to climb. This disease afflicts many Adventist churches, because they fail to provide for the ongoing spiritual development of their new people. They assume that each person can make it on his or her own, once baptized. This is a fatal error. If a church does not help people develop their spiritual life, ultimately a large segment of the church will be caught in "Adventism 101" and will fail to move on to deeper spiritual commitment. A church without deep spiritual commitment is a church headed for disaster. Therefore, this is a fatal illness.

## 8. ST. JOHN'S SYNDROME

McGavran called this disease St. John's Syndrome after John the Apostle. However, Adventists know the disease better by the term "Laodiceanism." Whereas arrested spiritual development is a disease afflicting primarily new Adventists, Laodiceanism afflicts old-time members. They are lukewarm—neither cold nor hot. God declares them to be disgusting in His sight. This disease, as we know, is very prevalent in the Adventist Church. As Ellen White declares:

> The message to the church of the Laodiceans applies especially to the people of God today. It is a message to professing Christians who have become so much like the world that no difference can be seen.[7]

Churches afflicted with this illness are filled with people who are nominal or cultural Adventists. They may have grown up Adventist and enjoy the culture and lifestyle, but they have no serious commitment to the fulfillment of the mission of Christ. They go through the motions of the church, but vibrant spiritual life is missing from the experience of these Laodicean members.

What is the remedy for this disease? The Holy Spirit. Only He can bring the needed revival to renew the church to find its spiritual moorings. It also helps if many new Christians are present. New Adventists are usually on fire for Christ. If there are enough of them around, the old Adventists caught up in Laodiceanism might recatch the wind of Holy Spirit power.

I was 17 and had just joined a small Adventist church of twenty-five members in a city of 50,000. Ten miles away was a city of 100,000, and we had no church there. I was excited about the message I had just accepted, but in the church were several Laodiceans who evidently were disturbed by my enthusiasm. I will never forget one dear old saint who approached me and put his arms around me and said: "Brother, you have your first-love experience. You just wait, and you will lose it like the rest of us!" If that is what happens to new people, no wonder Laodiceanism is a fatal disease for Adventists.

## CONCLUSION

Eight fatal diseases have been presented—and all are prevalent in the modern North American Adventist Church. If your church is afflicted with one or more diseases that are curable, then do something about it. We cannot afford to have churches lingering on life support and refusing the medicine God offers. As long as one of these diseases is afflicting your church, McGavran observed that the church will not grow.

So part of the process in dealing with creating a growing church is to remove those hindrances to growth so that nothing will block its progress. This is the essence of what Natural Church Development[8] has proposed. Remove the hindrances, and the church will grow all by itself. Create health, and the church will grow. This is why Natural Church Development is a return to the principles enunciated by McGavran in the early days of the church growth movement, before it was hijacked by the megachurch movement. This is why Natural Church Development resonates better with Adventists than does the information coming from the megachurch movement. It does not mean that we cannot learn something from the megachurches, but the basic principles of Adventism are far more in harmony with the early church growth movement and Natural Church Development than they are with the megachurch movement.

## Notes:

1. Wagner, C. Peter. *Your Church Can Grow* (Ventura, CA: Regal Publishing, 1984).

2. The principles enunciated in this section come from Donald McGavran. The comments on each principle are the words of the author.

3. Wagner, C. Peter. *Your Church Can Be Healthy* (Nashville, TN: Abingdon, 1979), 24-28.

4. For an extended discussion of McGavran's view of discipleship as the "initial bringing to Christ," along with the author's attempt to create a biblical definition of *disciple,* please consult the author's work, *Radical Disciples for Revolutionary Churches.*

5. The axioms enumerated here are attributable to Donald McGavran. The comments, however, belong to the author.

6. The names of the terminal illnesses are from Donald McGavran. The descriptions are in the words of the author, but their understanding has been gleaned from McGavran. See C. Peter Wagner. *Your Church Can Be Healthy.*

7. White, Ellen G. *Review and Herald,* August 20, 1903.

8. Natural Church Development refers to the biblical concepts developed by Christian Scwatz in his book, *Natural Church Development.* I have spoken much about it in previous books, and chapter 6 of this book will also deal with this concept.

# CHAPTER FIVE

# Church Growth Principles

A *church growth principle* is a universal truth about church growth that exists in every culture and group, whereas a *method* is a way a church applies a church growth principle. Many times churches confuse principles with methods. Some of the issues we have already examined in this book are really principles, such as developing a culture of evangelism. Utilizing laity and viewing evangelism as a process may also be considered solid principles that have been identified through the years by church growth scholars. In this chapter we wish to explore a few other principles recognized by church growth scholars as applicable in the church today.

## CHURCH GROWTH INVOLVES A UNION OF HUMAN AND DIVINE FORCES

When all has been written about church growth, one fact will never be altered: ultimately all church growth is attributable to God. He is the Empowerer of the church. Without His blessing all our human efforts cannot cause the church to grow. Church growth is a divine work. Yet God does not work independently of humans. For church growth to be effective, God and humanity work together. God did not commit the gospel commission to angels but to humans.

This is why the preaching of the gospel was committed to

erring men rather than to the angels. It is manifest that the power which works through the weakness of humanity is the power of God; and thus we are encouraged to believe that the power which can help others as weak as ourselves can help us.[1]

This does not diminish the fact that angels are working alongside us as we seek to fulfill the great commission, for it is a divine-human combination, but angels always put people in contact with God's church.

An angel guided Philip to the one who was seeking for light and who was ready to receive the gospel, and today angels will guide the footsteps of those workers who will allow the Holy Spirit to sanctify their tongues and refine and ennoble their hearts. The angel sent to Philip could himself have done the work for the Ethiopian, but this is not God's way of working. It is His plan that men are to work for their fellow men.[2]

This is the divine-human combination that God continually utilizes in His work with the human race. He demonstrated it in the person of Christ and continues to carry out this divine-human relationship as He seeks the salvation of the lost. The good news is that the church is not in the soul winning business alone. God is there. He is guiding the church for the accomplishment of His mission.

God is at work in our world. Jesus is drawing all people to Him. The Holy Spirit is the active agent of God directing the salvation enterprise. All three members of the divine Trinity are actively involved in the salvation of humans. At the same time, humanity must work in cooperation with this divine agency. Humans must have a right relationship with this God. They must have the right vision. They must have the right goals and tasks and be in the right time and place and reach the right people.

The right people are the people with whom God is working. We humans must be so in touch with our God that we hear Him speak, so that we work along the same lines that God is working. This is why spiritual focus is so crucial in the battle for the salvation of lost people. We have all heard stories such as that of a literature evangelist or pastor traveling down the road in a certain direction who feels a strong urge to turn around and go the opposite way. The person obeys the impulse and follows the leading of the Spirit. Somehow he manages to drive to a certain address, park the car, and walk up to an unknown door. When he knocks, the person opens the door with the news that she was praying that someone would come. That is the divine-human combination.

This is God and humanity working together. This is why spirituality can never be divorced from genuine soul winning. Soul winning and church growth can never be the performance of certain psychological tricks that cause people to become a part of the church of God. It is above all the work of a God with whom we Christians cooperate—a God who is passionate about using us to reach people who do not know Jesus.

## MEETING FELT NEEDS

A church can never grow beyond its ability to meet the felt needs of people. Churches that are serious about reaching people in today's sophisticated society are those that carefully understand the needs that exist in their community and reach out to meet those needs. The vast majority of unchurched people are never going to be reached if we don't first of all meet them at their point of need.

This is the essence of the Adventist holistic approach to evangelism that Ellen White so clearly annunciated. In her classic passage, she outlines what I often refer to as the "magna carta" of Adventist evangelism. It is a passage that I make every seminary student memorize, for it is the heart of her evangelistic understanding.

> Christ's method alone will give true success in reaching the people. The Saviour mingled with men as one who desired their good. He showed His sympathy for them, ministered to their needs, and won their confidence. Then He bade them, "Follow Me."[3]

Here Ellen White emphatically declares that this method alone will give true success in evangelism. This would indicate that other methods might give a false sense of success, but only Jesus' method will provide true success. And what was that method? Ellen White continues informing us that it was a relational, need-meeting approach that Jesus used. The only method that gives true success involves meeting people at the point of need.

Felt needs are absolutely essential. Any church utilizing any other approach as part of the process of evangelism is outside the will and plan of God. Ellen White continues in this passage to stress the importance of this approach in the personal realm rather than just in the corporate level. Notice her next words:

> There is need of coming close to the people by personal effort. If less time were given to sermonizing, and more time were spent

in personal ministry, greater results would be seen. The poor are to be relieved, the sick cared for, the sorrowing and the bereaved comforted, the ignorant instructed, the inexperienced counseled. We are to weep with those that weep, and rejoice with those that rejoice. Accompanied by the power of persuasion, the power of prayer, the power of the love of God, this work will not, cannot, be without fruit.[4]

What is indicated in the first statement is elaborated by the second. She is clearly talking about meeting felt needs. The servants of God must become close to the people they are trying to reach by meeting their needs. One cannot get close without spending time with the lost. Jesus was a great mingler, and Ellen White indicates that so must be God's church today. The members are salt and must permeate the community.

There is no call here to hibernate in the wilderness evangelizing jack rabbits. Here is an awesome invitation given by the prophet of the Lord to mingle, like Jesus, with the unlovely, the poor, and the lost. Jesus was friends with sinners. He attended their parties—met them where they were. Jesus never compromised His faith, but He loved to go where there were sinners. The people most comfortable around Jesus were sinners, while the ones most uncomfortable were the so-called saints. But Jesus didn't pay attention to that, because He had His priorities straight. He came to save sinners. That was His mission, and it should be our mission, even if we make some saints upset.

You cannot meet the needs of the people you are seeking to save unless you mingle with them and get acquainted with them. This is not a call to do a survey to find out needs. It is a clarion call for the church to obey the counsel of its prophet and get out of the fortress and mingle in the community. For too long Adventists have isolated themselves in safe havens and ghettos, as if the rest of the world did not exist. That time has ended. We cannot, we dare not, live in apostasy any longer. It is time to enter the community as individuals and as a church. We are not an isolated cult—we are the messengers of Jesus to a needy world that desperately needs to see authentic Christianity in action rather than be left to make decisions about Christianity based on portraits painted by the media.

George Barna once did some research indicating that many unchurched people said they did not know any Christians. No wonder they don't come to Jesus. The truth, however, may be that they *do* know

Christians, but those Christians have not identified themselves. What an indictment on believers. This does not mean we need to be out there publicly flaunting our faith before the world, but we need to be involved, and not in our cocoon, so that they see genuine Christianity in action.

It may be that we will have to go to some places where we are not comfortable, but so did Jesus. He visited the woman at the well; He found Mary Magdalene and brought her out of a den of iniquity; He befriended Matthew and Zachaeus—tax collectors—and then partied at their homes. That is the Jesus who calls us today to go and do likewise.

But someone will bring up the objection that if we attend parties with the lost, they might be serving alcohol—and then what will we do? Well, obviously, you don't need to drink the alcohol, but that does not prohibit you from attending. You can ask for a glass of 7-Up.

Joe Aldrich tells the story of a Baptist pastor who attended a neighborhood party where they served alcohol. His church took a strong stand on alcohol, but he still went to the party and drank his Sprite. As they were standing around the punch bowl, someone asked who they thought was the greatest person in the world. Wow, what an opportunity. He led three couples to Christ that night. However, when his church discovered that he had attended a party where alcohol was served, they fired him.[5] Are you willing to take that risk for Jesus?

In addition to personal involvement with the people in the community, the church must be involved corporately. This means being involved in community affairs; it means the pastor being in the local ministerial association; it means being involved with felt needs events happening in the community. It also means conducting seminars and other helpful outreaches for people in the community.

Yes, there is still room for the Community Service people to meet the needs of the homeless, hungry people in the community, but we must also meet other needs. God has equipped the Adventist Church with helpful insights in the areas of vegetarian cooking, parenting, stress, smoking cessation, etc. Conducting these kinds of seminars enables the church to build good relationships with people in the community and also to make strategic contacts that the church otherwise would not be able to make.

Here is a marvelous opportunity to get acquainted with people. Yet I have seen church after church conduct such seminars with no evangelistic, relational component. They simply put on the seminar for the community. The community folk sit in the front for the seminar while the church members gather at the back and watch—and never do the two meet. That is disgraceful, and it is not in harmony with God's counsel to mingle.

The whole purpose of conducting these seminars is to give church people a chance to mingle with unchurched people. In one church, we attempted to solve the problem. We were conducting a Five Day Plan to Stop Smoking. Rather than buddy the people with other smokers, I trained some of my members to be buddies. When a smoker came to the event, the person was immediately paired with one of our Adventist buddies, who sat beside them every night, gave them their phone number to call, and became their buddy. At the end of the seminar the participants had become deeply acquainted with their Adventist buddies. That provided a far better evangelistic opportunity than just helping them quit smoking. If you fail to build the relational component into these events, you will not be successful.

In the statement from *Ministry of Healing*, Ellen White emphatically declares that until you have met a person's needs, you have no right to address them spiritually. Where do we read in Scripture of button-holing people for Jesus or going up to strangers and asking if they are saved? No, the Bible and Ellen White are abundantly clear. We must first of all meet them at their point of need. Only then can we invite them to "Follow Jesus." This is a clear call for relational evangelism. Later on in this book we will explore the dynamics of relational evangelism, focusing on its application in friendship evangelism.

Once you have gained the confidence of people, it is much easier to share the gospel with them. Nothing is more obnoxious to unchurched people than these well-meaning Christians who will walk up to them or knock on their door to ask them if they are saved. I have talked to some who were so disgusted they quickly said yes to the invitation, not meaning it, just to get the person off their back. This is not evangelism—this is exploitation. It should not be found among those who are sharing the compassionate Christ with the people they meet. Rather than rushing to share Jesus or the Sabbath truth with people, first of all take time to get to know them. Then you will have won their confidence, and they will hear you. Otherwise, you are a clanging cymbal without light or heat.

Felt need relational evangelism is a strong principle of church growth. It is recognized not only by church growth scholars but is the heart of evangelism as understood by the prophet of the Lord to the Adventist

Church, Ellen White. Remember her declaration: only this method of evangelism will give true success. We dare not be delinquent here. We must utilize the relational approach in reaching lost people.

## NEW WAYS

Growing churches are willing to take risks to advance the cause of God. They are not afraid to try new ideas and discover new ways of working. The adage: "We don't do it that way here" finds no hearing in such churches. Because culture is constantly changing around us, the church must change its methodologies constantly in order to impact the community it is attempting to reach.

This does not mean that the church changes its message. Eternal truth is changeless, but how that truth is packaged will vary and change as the culture changes. Sometimes churches become so fearful of failure that they never attempt anything new. Such churches will surely fail. One church reported that three out of four things they tried failed, but they were not afraid to try the new idea. One church even reported that they gave an award each year to the person who came up with the best new idea that flopped. They wanted to encourage innovation and were not afraid to explore new ideas.

Long ago Ellen White counseled the Adventist Church constantly to find new methods and new ways of working. She was a great advocate of innovation in the Adventist Church. Sadly, many in the church today think they are following her counsel when they refuse to change, but a careful reading of her writings would indicate that their refusal to change methodologies is in direct disobedience to the prophet of the Lord. Read some of her counsel on innovation that I have selected below:

> In the cities of today, where there is so much to attract and please, the people can be interested by no ordinary efforts....Put forth extraordinary efforts in order to arrest the attention of the multitudes...Make use of every means that can possibly be devised for causing the truth to stand out clearly and distinctly.[6]

> The methods and means by which we reach certain ends are not always the same. [You] ...must use reason and judgment..."[7]

> Different methods of labor are to be employed to save different ones.[8]

> Different methods of labor are really essential.[9]

New methods must be introduced.[10]

God would have new and untried methods followed. Break in upon the people—surprise them.[11]

We must do something out of the common course of things. We must arrest the attention.[12]

Your efforts are too tame.[13]

As field after field is entered, new methods will come with the new workers who give themselves to the work. As they seek the Lord for help, He will communicate with them. They will receive plans devised by the Lord Himself.[14]

Church organization…is not to prescribe the exact way in which we should work.[15]

There must be no fixed rules; our work is a progressive work, and there must be room left for methods to be improved upon.[16]

Some of the methods used in this work will be different from methods used in the past, but let no one, because of this, block the way by criticism.[17]

There is to be no unkind criticism, no pulling to pieces of another's work.[18]

Can one find a stronger endorsement of innovation anywhere? The messenger of the Lord is abundantly clear. Methods change, but eternal truth never does. Churches that are serious about following the counsel of the Lord will constantly be attempting to discover new ways of working. New ideas, she declares, will especially come from the young adults who are new workers. Churches should be exceedingly careful not to stifle the new ideas coming from young adults. They may come up with better ideas to reach people. To hold them back and criticize their innovation is to stand in direct disobedience to the counsel of God. There are no fixed rules, she declares. Therefore all methodology is open to innovation. Don't be afraid to try something new for God.

## SUMMARY

In this chapter we have explored three more principles of growth that should encompass the planning of churches that are serious about reaching the lost. As they move forward, they will realize that they do not proceed in human strength, for church growth is a divine-human enterprise, with God and humanity working together. These churches, in obedience to Christ's method, will reach out and interact with their community, meeting the felt needs of the people so they earn the right to address them spiritually. They will be constantly innovating and trying new ideas, attempting to find a better way to reach earth's bulging population with heaven's final message.

## Notes:

1. White, Ellen G. *Desire of Ages* (Mountain View, CA: Pacific Press Publishing Association, 1940), 297.

2. White, Ellen G. *Acts of the Apostles* (Mountain View, CA: Pacific Press Publishing Association, 1911), 109.

3. White, Ellen G. *Ministry of Healing* (Mountain View, CA: Pacific Press Publishing Association, 1942), 143.

4. Ibid., 143, 144.

5. Aldrich, Joseph. *Gentle Persuasion* (Portland, OR: Multnomah Press), 195, 196.

6. White, Ellen G. *Testimonies for the Church*. vol. 9 (Mountain View, CA: Pacific Press Publishing Association, 1948), 109.

7. White, Ellen G. Gospel *Workers* (Washington, D.C.: Review and Herald Publishing Association, 1948), 468.

8. White, Ellen G. *Evangelism* (Washington, D.C.: Review and Herald Publishing Association, 1970), 166.

9. White, Ellen G. *Testimonies to Ministers* (Mountain View, CA: Pacific Press Publishing Association, 1962), 251.

10. White. *Evangelism*, 70.

11. Ibid., 125.

12. Ibid., 122, 123.

13. Ibid., 179.

14. White. *Testimonies for the Church*, vol. 6, 476.

15. Ibid., 116.

16. White. *Evangelism*, 105.

17. White. *Testimonies for the Church*, vol. 7, 25.

18. White. *Evangelism*, 106.

# CHAPTER SIX

# Natural Church Development

One of the most exciting developments in church growth over the last ten years has been the concept—and discoveries related to it—known as Natural Church Development (NCD). I consider Christian Schwarz's book on NCD to be the most significant book on church growth published in twenty-five years.[1, 2] In Chapter 4 we indicated that NCD brings the church growth movement back to the principles enunciated in the early days. These principles are much more in harmony with Adventist thinking. That is why the research here has received such warm reception in Adventism.[3]

I have referred to NCD in my other books. In *Waking the Dead*,[4] I shared some of the research we had discovered from surveys of Adventist churches in North America. In *Creating Healthy Churches Through Natural Church Development*,[5] I shared the Bible and Ellen White support for each of the principles of NCD. In this work, I wish briefly to review the eight quality characteristics and then share some of the results we are noticing in churches that are seeking health through NCD.[6]

## THE NCD THESIS

NCD operates on the premise that if a church is healthy, it will grow automatically. Therefore, rather than work on growth, the church seeks to bring itself to better health. When this happens, the church grows all by itself. This principle is found throughout nature. In nature, plants and animals do not grow by trying to grow. If they are healthy, they grow automatically. Good fruit occurs when there are good roots.

It is amazing how often Jesus utilized nature to explain the workings of the kingdom of God. "And why take ye thought for raiment? Consider the lilies of the field, how they grow; they toil not, neither do they spin: And yet I say unto you, that even Solomon in all his glory was not arrayed like one of these."[7] Jesus does not inform us to consider the beauty of the lilies but instead to study how they grow. They do not work at growing—if they are healthy, they grow automatically.

Again, Jesus illustrates the growth of the kingdom through natural means in the following passage:

> The kingdom of God is like a man who casts seed upon the soil, and goes to bed at night and gets up by day, and the seed sprouts up and grows—how: he himself does not know. The soil produces crops by itself; first the blade, then the head, then the mature grain in the head. But when the crop permits, he immediately puts in the sickle, because the harvest has come.[8]

This principle of automatic growth is found throughout Scripture. We do not understand how growth occurs. It just happens. The seed is buried in the earth, the rains come, the sun warms the soil, and suddenly the seed sprouts. So it is with the growth of the church. We plant the seed, but God waters it and sends the sun to warm it. As we cultivate the soil around the plant, it slowly matures until it is ready for harvest. This is one of the most basic principles of church growth, and, for that reason, I am taking a whole chapter on this principle.

Ellen White also firmly supports the concept that Jesus used this natural growth principle when dealing with people.

> And in dealing with men, He manifests the same principles that are manifest in the natural world. The beneficent operations of nature are not accomplished by abrupt and startling interpositions; men are not permitted to take her work into their own hands. God works through the calm, regular operation of His appointed laws. So it is in spiritual things. Satan is constantly seeking to produce effects by rude and violent thrusts; but Jesus

found access to minds by the pathway of their most familiar associations. He disturbed as little as possible their accustomed train of thought by abrupt actions or prescribed rules.[9]

Thus the principle laid down by NCD declares that a church should work on its health, and as it becomes healthy, it will grow automatically. As we have seen, this basic concept is supported by both the Bible and the writings of Ellen White. The unique help that NCD provides the church is not in the knowledge of the eight quality characteristics, identified by Schwartz, but in the fact that the organization provides an instrument that scientifically can measure the health of the church in all eight areas. This enables the church to work on its weak points with the clear knowledge that they have an accurate diagnosis of the problem. That always leads to good prescription. Before NCD arrived, churches could only guess at the problem and hope they had correctly identified it. Now we can know what the problems are and find good solutions that will enable the church to begin to grow in quality. Quality always produces quantity.

## THE EIGHT QUALITY CHARACTERISTICS[10]

Schwartz identifies eight quality characteristics that should be present in healthy churches. These eight quality characteristics for churches are like the eight natural remedies for physical health that Adventists often talk about. Now we have the eight natural remedies for church spiritual health. Schwartz's thesis is that the church's growth is impeded by the characteristic with the lowest score. Thus, as a church works on its health in that area, it will begin growing. Ideally, Schwartz discovered that when a church scores fifteen points above the norm, which is set at 50, it is always growing. Thus, a church would need a score of 65 in all the characteristics to have this enviable health. Few churches ever score that high in all the characteristics. In fact, in all the surveys we have conducted, we have only found a couple of Adventist churches scoring over 65 in all the characteristics. Thus, we all have room for growth.

## EMPOWERING LEADERSHIP

The first quality characteristic of empowering leadership indicates that a church utilizes its leadership to empower other people. The leaders of the church are not doing everything themselves—they are delegating and empowering the members of the church to be involved in the ministries of the church. With empowering comes equipping. So an empowering leader will be equipping the members so that they can be engaged in the ministry to which God has called them.

## GIFT-BASED MINISTRY

The second quality characteristic focuses on the people in ministry. Not only have they been empowered by the leadership, but they are actually utilizing their spiritual gifts in their ministry area. It is not enough simply to know what one's gifts are; one must also be deployed into a ministry that is utilizing one's spiritual gifts. It is not just ministry, but it is a ministry based on one's spiritual gifts.

## PASSIONATE SPIRITUALITY

Passionate spirituality produces contagious Christians. When one has a personal relationship with Jesus Christ, it produces a contented people who enjoy this dynamic friendship with Jesus. They joyfully display the contagious happiness that belongs to the followers of Jesus. Theirs is not a morbid Christianity but one that rejoices in all things, as Paul so aptly demonstrated in the Philippian jail. A church full of happy, contented Christians is a powerful drawing card.

## EFFECTIVE STRUCTURES

Effective structures occur when the boards, committees, and structures of the church are supporting the mission of the church. Churches with effective structures tie all their organizations to the accomplishment of their mission. They do not do things simply because they have always done them that way, but because they know the structure they have created will enable the church to accomplish its mission.

## INSPIRING WORSHIP SERVICES

Who would want uninspiring worship? Inspiring worship occurs only when the members have had an experience with Jesus during the week. Inspiring worship is not about putting cosmetic changes onto the church's worship service. Inspiring worship is a reflection of the inner joy of the worshipers because they have been with Jesus all week long. If religion is simply a once-a-week experience, then worship will be dull and barren of the Spirit of God. But when the members enjoy a vibrant relationship with God during the week, no matter what the style of the worship service, it will be inspiring. Inspiring worship is not about any particular style of worship. Instead, it is about authentic worship that connects with God.

## Holistic Small Groups

Holistic small groups does not refer to a church just having small groups. Some churches have small groups, but they are not holistic. A holistic group focuses on meeting the needs of the people both physically, mentally, and spiritually. These groups deal with one's whole being, not just the cognitive or mental area. They are a place where people can discuss their own personal struggles in an atmosphere of love and trust. They are not places to hang out all the dirty linen of one's life but rather are places where people are comfortable being themselves.

## Need-Oriented Evangelism

Need-oriented evangelism focuses on the needs of the people one is trying to reach. It does not ask them to be evangelized on our turf but seeks to reach them where they are, at their point of need. Ellen White's classic quotation from *Ministry of Healing,* page 143, which we examined earlier, is the heartbeat of Need-Oriented Evangelism. Quality churches are evangelistic congregations. They are passionate about reaching lost people and the priorities of the church demonstrate that commitment.

## Loving Relationships

The last quality characteristic is the crown jewel of what it means to be a Christian. Jesus declared this to be the defining characteristic of His disciples. Loving relationships are not optional for the church. It must radiate with love and acceptance. Too often the church has been quick to judge and slow to forgive, which is the opposite of the message of Jesus. He demonstrated and taught that we must forgive often and be careful not to judge one another. A church scoring high in Loving Relationships is a church that is demonstrating New Testament Christianity.

## Adventists and the Eight Characteristics

This quick overview of the eight quality characteristics indicates that each of these characteristics is absolutely essential for those churches that are serious about growth. We are not looking for growth for the sake of growth, but we desire healthy growth that produces people who are ready to meet Jesus at His coming. So if your church is desirous of growth, then consider utilizing the NCD principles and begin the journey to better health. Along the way you will experience better growth automatically.

The North American Division Evangelism Institute has on record the results of the NCD survey from hundreds of Adventist churches in North America. From this data, trends have clearly emerged. The two characteristics that Adventist churches seem to score highest in are Need-Oriented Evangelism and Passionate Spirituality. The average scores in these two areas are very close to each other, and these are the only two characteristics where the Adventist average is above the norm of 50. Of course, many churches score much higher, while others score far below, but on average these are the highest.

The two characteristics that Adventists score worst in are Inspiring Worship Services and Holistic Small Groups. Inspiring Worship scores are very close to the middle of the range of characteristics, right below Gift-Based Ministry scores, but Holistic Small Groups has consistently scored very low. In other words, there is a large gap between the scores for Inspiring Worship and Holistic Small Groups. Holistic Small Groups averages a score of only 39, while Inspiring Worship and Gift-Based Ministry are nearly tied at 42. In contrast, Passionate Spirituality and Need-Oriented Evangelism are nearly tied at 51, with only fractions separating them.

## Growth and Health in Adventist Churches

Adventist churches that are healthy report a much higher rate of annual growth than those that are not as healthy. The NCD study asks pastors to record their church attendance as part of the survey. This means that the results are not based on membership but on attendance growth and are also are dependent on what each pastor reported. There is no way to be certain that pastors have not estimated their attendance incorrectly in either direction. These variables must be acknowledged as we analyze the data.

Here are the results. In Adventist churches scoring an average NCD score of 35 or under, pastors are reporting an annual growth rate of 9.34 percent in attendance. (These would be the churches that are in the poorest health.) Overall, 20.5 percent of Adventist churches score in this area.[11]

The medium range of health is where 76.4 percent of all Adventist churches are falling. They score an average on the NCD scale that is between 36 and 64 and report an annual attendance growth of 10.15 percent. However, churches scoring an average that is above 65 on the scale, which comprise only 3.1 percent of Adventist churches, are reporting an annual attendance growth of 21.75 percent.

These figures which pastors have reported clearly indicate the relationship between health and growth. A fascinating observation is that the attendance growth pattern in the low and medium categories of health is not significantly different. It is obvious that outstanding attendance growth only kicks in when the average score for a church is over 65. This decisively demonstrates that there is a connection between health and growth. Churches that are healthy simply grow faster in attendance than those that are not as healthy.

We have also examined the profiles of those churches that have done two NCD surveys. Of these churches, 65 percent have actually increased their score (9.6 points on the average), while 35 percent of the churches filling out a second survey actually decreased their score. Obviously, some churches worked on health, while others just took a survey. Those that worked effectively on their problem areas actually improved their health.

In examining those churches that took two profiles (this includes both those that improved and those that did not) we have discovered that overall, they average an increase in attendance. For example, in the first profile the average was 137 adults per church in attendance. In the second survey, these same churches averaged 145 adults in attendance. Significantly, the average membership in these churches declined from 273 to 266 members. Thus the rate of attendance to membership increased from 52 percent to 56 percent. What is most remarkable is that the churches reported a whopping increase in the attendance of children. Amazingly, they reported a 50 percent increase in the number of children that turned out for church. In addition, the annual attendance growth rate for these churches increased six times between the two profiles, from 2.3 percent to 12.5 percent.

We currently have 31 churches that have taken a third survey. Here, the trends begin to become very noticeable. In this group of churches, 16.1 percent were declining churches. Their quality score actually decreased by 10.1 percent, on average, while their attendance also declined by 10.3 percent and their membership by 3 percent. When the quality goes down, it definitely affects the growth.

In this same group, 22.6 percent of the churches taking the third survey are considered plateued in quality—just holding their own. Their quality only declined by ½ percent, but their attendance went up 7.1 percent, and membership increased by 14.2 percent. Even those Adventist churches that maintained quality at the exact same level continued to see some growth.

However, the most spectacular growth was seen in the 61.5 percent of these churches that increased their quality between the first and third surveys. Their average increase was 13.1 percent in quality, while at the same time revealing a 19.7 percent increase in attendance and a 15.2 percent increase in membership. Once again, the data is clearly revealing the relationship between improving quality and church growth. Any church concerned about growth must also be concerned about improving church health.

While the actual numbers may have some exaggeration in them, the overall trend is quite consistent. Churches that are improving in health are increasing the attendance of the congregation. This would suggest that the key element in creating a growing church would be to measure the health of the church through the NCD process. This will allow the church to work effectively on improving its health. The more Adventist churches follow this pattern, the faster they will grow.

What we are advocating here is not just growth in numbers but holistic growth. Church life must improve, and church growth will follow. Qualitative growth precedes quantitative growth. The NCD process is an excellent tool to help a church actually measure its health and improve in quality. When it does, the church will begin to grow automatically.

**Notes:**

1.  Schwartz, Christian, *Natural Church Development* (Carol Stream, IL: ChurchSmart Resources, 1996).

2.  Schwartz, Christian, *Color Your World With NCD* (Charles, IL: ChurchSmart Resources, 2005).

3.  The two books on NCD are essential for understanding the concepts. *Natural Church Development* is the original book that reports on the initial findings. *Color Your World With NCD* is an updated and expanded version of the research, bringing one up to date with what has happened

in NCD since the original book was published.

4. Burrill, Russell. *Waking the Dead* (Hagerstown: Review and Herald, 2004).

5. Burrill, Russell. *Creating Healthy Adventist Churches Through Natural Church Development* (Berrien Springs: NADEI, 2003).

6. Even though the words in this chapter are those of the author, he wishes to express his indebtedness to the materials published by the NCD organization for the information and basic concepts explored by the author in this work.

7. Matthew 6:28, 29.

8. Mark 4:26-29.

9. White. *Testimonies to Ministers*, 189, 190.

10. For a more detailed description and analysis of each of the eight quality characteristics, the reader is referred to the book *Color Your World With NCD,* by Schwartz—and to *Creating Healthy Adventist Churches Through Natural Church Development,* by the author. The description that follows is meant to provide a very brief overview of the eight quality characteristics.

11. It is obvious from the numbers that the report on attendance is probably exaggerated some. However, it should be noted that there is a clear relationship between health and growth, even if some pastors have been overly optimistic in their attendance reporting.

# CHAPTER SEVEN

# Reaching Friends for Jesus

In an earlier chapter we explored the need for the church to practice Ellen White's concept of meeting felt needs.[1] Only in a relational setting does one have the right to address people spiritually. A relational style of evangelism is therefore essential if the church desires to follow the counsel of Ellen White. Interestingly, in the research my students have done examining churches that are growing through convert growth, they have also discovered that many of them utilize friendship evangelism as a key component of the growth process.

The world is different today than it was prior to the 1960s. The 60s witnessed a transformation in society. The pre-60s world in North America was one in which there were stable families, close family ties, and a non-mobile society. In the pre-60s world, people lived and died in the same community. Few people moved far from where they were born. Relational needs of people were being met by family and community.

My own family is an example of the non-mobility of people. For 300 years my ancestors had lived in northeastern Massachusetts. Then my generation moved out. Today, I know of no relatives (there may be some I don't know) who still live in northeastern Massachusetts. The stability created by living for generations in the same community is gone in twenty-first century North America.

The 60s also witnessed a very confrontational society. Those coming of age at this time questioned everything—from the lack of civil rights to the foundational mores of society. Even in the church, the standards and mores of the church were questioned by this generation emerging in the 1960s. As a result, the world has greatly changed, and we now live in a different cultural world than the pre-60s era.

What is this new cultural society? Today, there is a new definition of family. Rather than a family being considered as mother, father, and children, today it may be: mother and children, father and children, mother-mother and children, father-father and children, or even grandparents and children. From gay marriages to couples living together without marriage, we now live in a strange new world.

In the pre-60s era families usually stayed together. Divorce was uncommon. It may not have meant the marriage was wonderful, but respect for the marriage institution prevented many divorces. Today, children are the products of multiple marriages. Often custody arrangements necessitate that children are transferred back and forth between parents, sometimes without regard for the emotional health of the family. As a result, children are maturing without a stable environment, and this has serious consequences for the future of society.

The twenty-first century is emerging as the urbanized society. In 1900 only 20 percent of America was urbanized, but today the figure is nearly 80 percent. The closer people live together, the less they know each other. When people lived in rural communities, everyone knew everything about everyone else, but in a city, you are lucky if you even know the name of the person on the other side of the wall. Thus, people are relationally starved.

Add to that the mobility of our sophisticated twenty-first century, and one soon notices that instability has become the norm. No one even dares to build deep relationships with people, for fear of the loss when they move the next time. Consequently, many people have only shallow relationships. Sometimes, if you befriend a person, they will quickly tell you that you are their best friend. This lack of commitment and instability of people in relationships has created a new kind of society—one that desperately needs relational bonding.

Relational needs that were formerly met by community and relatives are no longer being satisfied. Many people do not have a support network, and they are starved, relationally. If ever there were an age in which the church needed to step in and fill relational needs, it is today.

In earlier times it was not a vital issue, but at present, the church is one of the only places left where people can bond together. The alternatives are the corner bar or nightclub—Satan's counterfeits for the church. Now is the time for the church to follow the counsel of Ellen White and develop a relationally built ministry.

A friendship approach to evangelism suggests that the church become serious about meeting people's relational needs, as the first step to reaching them. Building solid friendships with unchurched people is no longer an option for Seventh-day Adventists—it has become a vital necessity.

## OIKOS EVANGELISM

The New Testament strategy of evangelism is apparent throughout the story of the early church. There may have been a few great preachers, such as Peter and Paul, but the fantastic growth of the early church was due to the individual witness of the early Christians who shared Christ among the people they knew. This is called "oikos" evangelism.

*Oikos,* a Greek word meaning "household" is used to describe the methodology of the early church in sharing Christ among the people they knew. It is not a reference merely to people who lived in the same house but to those who had common ties and tasks with existing believers.[2] It is the most common method of sharing Christ that one discovers in the New Testament era.

Let's notice a few examples of oikos evangelism in the New Testament. In Acts 16, we find the story of Paul's establishing the church at Philippi. On Sabbath Paul goes to the riverside, where he meets Lydia and shares the good news of Jesus with her. However, Paul does not just baptize Lydia—the Bible declares that he baptized her and her household (oikos).[3] Later on in the chapter, Paul and Barnabas witness the miraculous conversion of the Philippian jailer. After the jailer invites Paul and Barnabas to spend the night at his house, the next morning Paul baptizes not just the jailer, but his oikos.

In Luke 19, the physician tells the story of the conversion of Zacchaeus. No sooner does the tax collector come down from the sycamore tree than Jesus informs him that salvation has come to his oikos.[4] Not only was Zacchaeus converted, but his conversion provided entry to the rest of his oikos. If Zacchaeus had not come to Christ, he would not have been a witness to his household. Every person converted brings with them an oikos that can now be reached because of the new convert.

Another powerful example is the story of the healed demoniac.[5] Here is a wild man whom no one could tame—a man whose life was totally taken over by demons. No sooner is he converted than Jesus informs him that he is to return to his oikos to share the good news of what Jesus has done for him. If there were ever anyone unfit to witness, this was the man. He had not even heard a sermon from the lips of the Savior, but he is immediately commissioned to go forth to his oikos.

Oikos evangelism is not only the best methodology for reaching people today, it is the methodology endorsed by Jesus and the early church. How we go about it might be different, but it is a God-given approach that resulted in the superlative growth of the early church. It still works today.

I was sitting at my desk in the church office when two strangers walked in. They had recently become Adventists and were concerned that their daughter, who lived near our church, also be exposed to the Adventist message. It was summertime, and Vacation Bible School (VBS) was approaching. They asked if I would see that their grandchildren at least got invited to VBS. I gladly told them we would do it and passed the name on to our VBS leader, who promptly placed the name on top of her refrigerator and forgot it.

After VBS was over and she was cleaning house, she discovered the name. Being a very conscientious person, she felt bad about forgetting, but she did not stop there. She went out to visit the woman. She found a drunk—consumed with alcohol. Her children were running wild around the neighborhood, while her 17-year old son was living in the house with his girlfriend.

Rather than being discouraged by the sight she beheld, the VBS leader offered to come and give her Bible studies. The daughter agreed. Months later, the leader invited her to an evangelistic meeting, where she gave her heart to Jesus and was baptized. However, the story didn't end there. After her baptism, a neighbor was visiting with her and commented about her changed life. "Your kids used to be the terror of the neighborhood," she declared, "but now they are different. What happened?"

As she shared her faith with her neighbor, it led to more Bible studies and the baptism of her neighbor and ultimately, the neighbor's husband. As news spread of the changed lives, other neighbors were baptized—and even her son and his live-in girlfriend were married and baptized. Ultimately twenty-five people were baptized from this one contact—and all because of a misplaced invitation to VBS! This is oikos evangelism at its very best.

Research has suggested that up to 70 percent of people who join the church do so through a friend or relative, although the research in the Adventist Church indicates that the percentage is nearer to 60 percent.[6] Still, it is the most common way people come to Christ and the church. This is what is happening, without the church even attempting to tap into the networks of people that new members know. What would happen if this whole approach were made intentional and deliberate?

## The Extended Congregation

Years ago Win Arn[7] suggested that the name for this phenomenon is the "extended congregation." He discovered that the average church member has a relationship with between six and nine unchurched persons. I have discovered that outside Adventist centers, it can actually be as high as ten to twelve unchurched people that members know. All the unchurched friends and family of the members are thus called the *extended congregation.* It is this pool from which most of the new converts to the church will come. Since we know who these people are, it would make sense to focus our ministry on reaching this group of the most receptive people in our community.

If a church had 100 members, and each member could identify six or eight unchurched friends and family members, then the extended congregation of that church would be 600 to 800 people. It would then make sense to focus most of the ministry activity of the church on these people who are already connected to existing church members. With this understanding, a church would then look at itself as a church of 700 to 900 instead of 100—the members of the extended congregation being added to the church. Of course, we are not suggesting that they be added to the membership roles (not yet, at least!) but only in the thinking of the church, as it plans its ministry around the needs of this new understanding of the congregation.

Imagine a church that is truly being intentional about reaching the family and friends of its members. In such a church, the members would have personally identified many of the people in their extended family who do not know Jesus. There would be a mechanism in the church whereby they could let the church know the demographic information of these people: their marital status, the children, the ages, the interests, the needs, etc.

Having received all this information, the church would then plan its activities around the needs of the unchurched friends and families of its members. With events being planned around those needs, the members will feel good about inviting their friends and family to the events. Ideally, every event the church conducts is a possibility for inviting people from the extended family to enjoy the event with the members.

If the church is having a music concert, the members would not just invite other Adventists but also the members of their extended family. When the church has a campout, the extended congregation is invited to join, if they have an interest in camping. If the church has a social event, the members invite the extended congregation. No matter what the event, it is planned with the invitation of the extended family in mind.

In addition, as data is collected on the extended congregation, specific events are designed especially to meet their needs, so they begin to come to a multitude of events sponsored by the church. What we are attempting to do is to fellowship them before attempting to share the message. Once they feel part of our fellowship, teaching the message to them will be simple.

Can you imagine the excitement in the church as the members witness the extended congregation being baptized into the real congregation? The morale of such a church would escalate with the excitement that comes from seeing friends and family becoming part of God's church. This is not an approach that simply wishes members would invite their friends and family—it is an approach where all the activities of the church are planned with the extended congregation in mind.

Imagine two churches—one that is conscious of the extended congregation, and one that is concerned only about the existing members. Both churches play basketball in the church gym. One church has a rule that you have to be a member of the church to play on the basketball team. The other church has a rule that you can play only if you bring an unchurched friend with you. Which church is focused on the extended congregation? The answer is obvious.

The church is not an exclusive club for members only. Someone has suggested that the church is a fishing vessel and not a luxury cruise liner. Fishing vessels can be messy. The fish are caught, thrown on the deck, their guts are cut out, and the smell is not the best. On a luxury cruise liner, the deck is immaculate, and everything is in order. If you brought your fishing pole to the luxury cruise liner and started fishing off the deck and throwing the fish on board, you would be stopped before the fish hit the deck. They don't want the place messed up with newly caught fish. What kind of church do you attend? It is to be hoped that your church is a fishing vessel and not a private luxury cruiser.

When a church practices Christ's method of evangelism, as espoused by Ellen White,[8] it will indeed be a fishing vessel, the members mingling with the unchurched, building relationships with them, and earning the right to share the gospel. Churches that focus on the extended congregation will encourage their members regularly to build relationships with unchurched people.

Building such relationships will mean doing things together—eating together, enjoying common sports together, etc. If a church member discovers that an unchurched friend likes to go fishing, he will go fishing with his friend, even if he doesn't enjoy fishing. He goes because he is focused on building a relationship with this person. It may also help to invite another church friend along who does enjoy fishing. That way, the unchurched person gets acquainted with more than one church member.

The same would hold true for any event. Perhaps it is golfing or shopping or some sporting event that the unchurched person enjoys. Then the church member will go with him or her. Obviously, church members would not go to places where they would compromise their faith, but there are many activities that families and individuals enjoy doing regardless of their religious status. Attending such events only opens the door for the opportunity to share.

Ultimately, there arises a need in the unchurched person's life. Maybe some unwanted health news—or an auto accident that puts them into the hospital. In the moment of crisis they are apt to call their friend, who then has a wonderful opportunity to minister to them during their time of need. At such times people are more open and receptive to spiritual truth. However, since it is being done in the setting of a relationship, the church member should always ask permission to share. For example, in their crisis a person mentions that his or her life seems so empty. The church member responds and shares that one time, she felt the same way in her life, but Christ has now given real meaning to her life. Then she asks, "Would you like me to share with you what happened that changed my life?" With a positive response, the church member begins to share her faith and work into a gospel presentation that could ultimately end with the friend giving his or her life to Jesus.

This sharing is being done in the context of a relationship. It is one friend telling another about what a precious Friend they have found in Jesus. It should never be forced, but the invitation can be freely shared at the right opportunity in the person's life. At this point, one would not share the distinctive doctrines of the Adventist faith. That can come later. Unchurched people must first be brought to Jesus. Once they accept Jesus, they obviously will want to attend church with their friend, and there will be plenty of time for them to learn the doctrines.

Our whole focus in friendship evangelism is building relationships with all these unchurched people. The tie to the church becomes even stronger if, along the way and before the crisis comes, the church member has invited the friend to many church events. Attendance at any of these events could spark some leading questions that would enable the church member to share, even without a crisis event. This is why inviting people to church events, along with building relationships, is the key to friendship evangelism

Some have thought they were doing friendship evangelism simply by witnessing non-verbally to their friends. They do not intentionally attempt to share but simply declare that their life is a witness. That is not friendship evangelism. Friendship evangelism is a definitive strategy to build relationships with unchurched people and invite them to church events so we earn the right to share Jesus at the appropriate time.

One caution: friendship is not bait with which to hook our friends into religion. We build relationships with unchurched people because that is what Jesus did. As a result of those relationships, people come to Christ, but if they do not, we do not drop them as friends. Our friendships with people must be genuine and not just ploys to get them into the church. Yet when Christians build such relationships, people indeed do come to Christ and the church.

Churches utilizing the friendship approach to evangelism will have activities constantly happening so that church members can regularly invite their friends to attend. Friendship evangelism churches will also regularly conduct public meetings to which the members can invite both friends and relatives. In our research we have noted that churches using friendship evangelism exclusively, without adding the public evangelism component, rarely are successful. As in all areas of outreach, the reaping event is what brings it together and creates the harvest.

## PROFILE OF THE NEW CONVERT WHO STAYS

Several years ago some interesting research was conducted by Flavil Yeakley[9] on the differences between converts, drop-outs, and those who did not join the church but were exposed to it. He examined 240 people in each category and then developed what was called the profile of the new convert who stays. While the research is not recent, it still has tremendous value, and the author has seen it vindicated numerous times over the years.

Yeakley enunciated seven points that describe the new convert who stays.

### 1. New converts have multiple exposures to the church.

An exposure would be some contact a person has with the church. It might be a friend in the church who is close to them, a Vacation Bible School experience, a Bible course, an evangelistic meeting, a felt need seminar, etc. The more of these exposures a person has, the better their chance of joining the church and staying with the church. Yeakley discovered that the converts averaged 8.6 contacts, while the dropouts had 2.2, and the non-converts less than two contacts.[10] This strongly suggests what we talked about earlier in this book. Evangelism is a process. That is why multiple exposures are so crucial.

The Engel scale (below and on the following page) has often been used by church growth scholars to demonstrate that evangelism is a process that begins before conversion and continues afterward.

-8   Awareness of a Supreme Being, but no Effective Knowledge of the Gospel

-7   Initial Awareness of Gospel

-6   Awareness of the Fundamentals of the Gospel

-5   Grasp of the Implications of the Gospel

-4   Positive Attitude Toward the Gospel

-3   Personal Problem Recognition

-2   Decision to Act

-1   Repentance and Faith in God
     NEW CREATURE

+1   Post-Decision Evaluation

+2   Incorporation Into the Church Body

+3   Conceptual and Behavioral Growth

+4   Communion With God

+5   Stewardship

+6   Reproduction

+7   Internally (Spiritual Gifts, etc)

+8   Externally (Witness, Social Action, etc.)[11]

## 2. New converts view their conversion as non-manipulative.

How the new converts perceive their conversion process is indica-
tive of whether they stay with the church or leave. Yeakley suggested
three views by which churches attempt to transmit the gospel to new
people.[12] The first is called the Information Transmission model. This
view of giving the gospel operates on the assumption that the gospel
is primarily informational. If the right information is conveyed, then
people will make a decision. For example, a church member hears a
powerfully clear presentation on the seventh-day Sabbath. She walks
out of the meeting and declares that if only her friend had heard that
presentation, she knows she would have accepted it, because it was so
clear.

However, most people have no problem with the clarity of the
Sabbath—the problem lies more with what friends and family may
think, or maybe with a job. So, no matter how much more information
one gives, decisions still will not occur. The research discovered that 75
percent of the people approached this way will say No.[13] So you need to
go through a lot of people to get a few converts.

As Adventists, we have had a tendency to overuse this approach. We
will even refer to accepting the "message" or how long have you been in
the "truth." We Adventists have great information, and information is
needed in gospel witness, but the gospel is shared by more than information. So we need to explore models other than a mere cognitive approach of sharing with our friends in hopes of bringing them to Christ
and the church.

The second model of gospel transmission is called Manipulative
Monologue. This view sees the process as somewhat manipulative. The
tactics of high pressure salesmanship are at the heart of the approach
employed here in sharing the gospel. I once worked with an evangelist

who utilized this approach. I remember sitting in a home as he told the couple that if they did not decide to be baptized right then, they would be lost eternally. That is high pressure and uncalled for by true disciples of Jesus. Jesus never put high pressure on anyone.

Does it work? Ask any good salesperson. That is why it is used in sales, but the gospel is not for sale. You do not need to use high pressure to win people to Jesus. The research revealed, however, that 81 percent of the people approached with high pressure will say Yes. That is why it is so tempting to use this method. It gets results. However, the research also discovered that one year later 85 percent of the 81 percent who said Yes will have left the church.[14] So this approach primarily produced dropouts.

The third approach is the friendship or relational approach, called the Non-Manipulative Dialogue model. This view recognizes that no two people ever see things exactly the same way. It doesn't mean one does not try to influence the other, but such sharing is always being done in the context of a relationship. That is the approach we have been suggesting in this chapter.

The results of utilizing this model are spectacular—99 percent of those approached in a friendship model will ultimately say Yes, and one year later, 96 percent of these will still be active. The evidence is overwhelming for a friendship approach to evangelism. And even when we use the traditional Bible study or public meeting, it has to be combined with a friendship approach if it is to truly produce disciples of Jesus.

Another interesting finding from Yeakley's research is that in churches with high growth, the pastor viewed evangelism as Non-Manipulative Dialogue, but when the pastor viewed evangelism as Manipulative Monologue, it primarily produced medium growth, and when the pastor viewed evangelism as Information Transmission, it produced low growth.

The research further examined how church members viewed evangelism. When the church members viewed evangelism as Information Transmission, it primarily produced non-converts. Likewise, when the church members were into Manipulative Monologue, it produced dropouts, but when the church members viewed evangelism as Non-Manipulative Dialogue, it produced converts.

One further analysis looked at how the person regarded his persuader. The non-converts saw the persuader as a teacher, the dropouts as a salesperson, but the converts—by a wide margin—saw the persuader as a friend. All of this clearly suggests that churches that are serious about keeping people need to be employing the Non-Manipulative Dialogue model.[15]

**3. New converts who stay have recently experienced a high degree of change in their life situation.**

The more change a person is experiencing in life, the more open and receptive that person is to a new orientation of life. Thus, conversion is more apt to occur as a result of multitudinous changes occurring at the same time. Of course, change in the life does not bring conversion. Many converted people facing change end up leaving the church. Change provides openness to new ideas that did not exist without the change.

There are certain times in the life cycle when more change is occurring. The most open and receptive period in the adult life cycle is between 18 and 30 years of age. This is the period when a person gets married, has children, experiences financial status changes, gets a job, moves out on their own, etc. Most people convert during these years. The older people get, the less responsive they are to accepting Jesus. Each succeeding period is less open and receptive.

The second-most open and receptive period is between 45 and 50, when the children leave the home or mid-life crisis occurs. The third period is when one retires, around 65. Many times retirees move to a new area, creating an openness. The final period is at the death of a spouse. Again, this does not mean conversion will happen at this time, but this is when it is more likely to occur. In fact, the higher the amount of change, the more likely a new orientation to life will occur.

Let me illustrate with my own conversion story. I was raised as a devout member of the Baptist Church (American Baptist). My father was a "born a Baptist, going to die a Baptist" kind of guy. Early on in life I had decided to become a pastor. By 13, I was already teaching younger children in Sunday School. I knew nothing about Seventh-day Adventists. The Adventist Church in my Massachusetts town had twenty-five members and was on the opposite side of town from where I lived, so I had no contact.

When I was 14, I had my own paper route. Amazingly, I had three Adventist families on my route. And they were my worst customers!

Friday night was collection night, and they would never pay on Sabbath, so I had to collect from them at another time, and it was frustrating. I did not understand their convictions.

It was a Friday night, March 9—snow and ice were still on the roads and pathways of this New England town. I was one home away from an Adventist home. The sun was sinking in the west. I knew that if I wanted to get paid that night, I needed to hurry to get to the Adventist home. After collecting, I raced to the Adventist home, but ended up slipping on a piece of ice, falling and breaking my leg in two places —and all because of these crazy Adventists!

In those days, you were laid up for three months in bed waiting for the leg to heal—quite a frustration for an active teenager. Since I was confined to bed on Sunday mornings, I was unable to go to church, so I did the next best thing: I turned on the radio and listened to some religious programs. One interesting program began with: "Lift up the Trumpet, and Loud Let it Ring." This speaker, H. M. S. Richards, opened the Bible and made it live. And then the program offered a Bible course. I thought it would be an excellent way to help prepare me to be a Baptist preacher, so I wrote to the Voice of Prophecy and began taking their Bible course, little realizing what I was getting into.

When I came to the Sabbath lessons, I began to see the connection with the people on my paper route, but by then I was hooked. I wrote the Voice of Prophecy many questions, and they always took the time to biblically answer the questions of a 14-year old. Later that summer, the Adventist pastor came to visit me, and I started attending church by myself.

However, my Baptist father quickly discerned my interests and did not want his son entangled with this obscure religion. So he moved the family from Massachusetts to Florida to get us away from the Adventists, little realizing that there were more Adventists in Florida than in Massachusetts.

When we arrived in Florida, I had somewhat convinced my mother of the Sabbath, so she started accompanying me to church on Sabbath, but my dad was opposed. After three weeks of Sabbath attendance, he forbade us to go to church. Since only he could drive, that ended our Sabbath experience in Florida. He tried desperately to find a Baptist church we would be happy in, but to no avail, for all the Baptist church-es there were Southern Baptists, and they were quite different from the American Baptist church we attended in Massachusetts.

After six months and three moves in Florida, he moved us back to Massachusetts, hoping that we would feel at home back in the old Baptist church there. No sooner did we arrive than it was discovered that the pastor, whom my father loved and respected, was having an affair with a church member and was dismissed. This devastated my dad, and from then on, he allowed us to go to the Adventist church each Sabbath. We no longer attended the Baptist church, but my mother, brother, and I attended the small Adventist church on Sabbath, while my dad would go to the library to find ammunition he could use against us.

Slowly, his opposition lessened. Perhaps what he was reading in the library was slowly leading him into the church. On the first Sabbath in January 1958, my dad walked out of the bedroom, dressed in his suit, and announced that he was going to find out about those "Advents" firsthand. He never missed another Sabbath. He was born a Baptist, but died an Adventist literature evangelist.

As my story indicates, much change was occurring in my young adolescent life, beyond the usual changes in the body of a teenager. This massive amount of change made it possible for us as a family to be open enough to accept Adventism. Perhaps if I had never broken my leg and been confined to bed, I never would have listened to the Voice of Prophecy and would not be writing this book today. Change in the life is a major factor in the openness of people.

## 4. New converts who stayed developed relationships with church members prior to conversion.

It is amazing how many of the issues of retention hinge on developing relationships with people. The research here indicated that converts had built relationships with church members, not just after conversion but also before conversion. People rarely join a church where they do not know the people.[16] This means that a person's retention begins with the first contact that a person has with the church.

One cannot wait until a person makes the decision to join the church. One must begin building relationships from the moment of first contact. This means that even in our public meetings, time must be built in for relational bonding to occur. In my meetings, we utilize the row host system, and we have a refreshment time after the meeting. This enables people to stand around and socialize after a meeting and thus begin the process of building relationships.

### 5. New converts have friendships in the church.

This point is closely related to the previous point. The difference is that not only do people need relationships and friendships before entering the church, they also need it after they have joined the church. In fact, Yeakley's research revealed that new converts needed to have at least seven friends in the church during their first six months as members. Rarely, if ever, do people leave, who develop such a number of relationships. In fact, the research actually suggested that this was the strongest factor in keeping new members.[17]

How can one develop seven friendships in the church in six months? It will not happen if the only exposure is Sabbath morning worship! A friend is defined as someone I have contact with *outside of* Sabbath morning. This necessitates the new convert being involved in some small group. Small groups are the key to retention. Rarely, if ever, does the church lose a person who becomes involved in a small group.

Yet small groups continue to be a hard sell to many Adventist congregations. Members—who already have built good relationships in the church—see no need. My plea is to remember that new people need these more than old members. Yet, I also believe old members would be stronger if they were involved in a small group. I do not want to be redundant with what I have written in other books, so I would refer the reader to my book that explains the absolute need for a small group ministry.[18] Small group involvement is not optional; it is mandatory for any church that is concerned about keeping new members.

### 6. New converts who stayed fit in the church.

Not only have the new converts who stayed built relationships in the church, but Yeakley's research also revealed that the people of the church were similar to them in age and socio-economic status. Someone may object that all people are equal.[19] This is true, but people still are more apt to join a church if the people there are more like themselves.

In the research, Yeakley discovered that the closer in age and socio-economic status the church was to the community, the faster that church was able to grow. The assumption is that when people joined the church, they felt at home. If they join a church where they don't fit, they are not likely to stay for long.

Regarding age differential, it was discovered that growing churches were only 2.9 years different from the community median age, while plateaued churches had a 7.7-year disparity from the community, and declining churches revealed an 11.9-year differential. That is why a church of senior citizens cannot attract young people to their church. The age difference is too wide. So what can you do? You can't change the ages of your members. The only solution is to hope that there is someone of similar age in your church who can befriend the new member. If the church has no one who can do so, the new member will probably not stay. In fact, if there is another Adventist church nearby where the person would fit better, it would be best to suggest that the individual attend there. Of course, you are thinking, we need the young person. Remember, it is not *your* needs that count—it is the retention of the new person for the kingdom of God.

A second area pointed out was the socio-economic difference. The socio-economic scale has nine parts: lower lower, middle lower, upper lower, lower middle, middle middle, upper middle, lower upper, middle upper, and upper upper. The research pointed out that growing churches are one-half step above the community. People want to feel they are moving up the socio-economic scale when they join a church. Plateaued churches average one-half step below the community, while the declining church average plus or minus two points in either direction.[20]

What this reveals is that when people join a church, they enjoy being around people who have similar interests, outside of religion. To bond and build relationships, it is essential that the church be able to relate to all groups of people. Again, we cannot change who we are, but we can be cognizant of the need to help people who join us and are different in these areas. If we are serious about keeping new converts in the church, we should be aware that some need extra special attention.

### 7. New converts have been integrated into a group, role, or task.

The final issue also revolves around the need of new converts to develop relationships. They must be involved in some group or given some role or task in the church, and this must be done in the first six months of their membership. You might not make them head elder, but you certainly must involve them in some ministry. Until people contribute their time to the church, the church does not belong to them. Once they give of themselves, their language changes. They no longer talk about "your church"—it now becomes "my church."

As noted in the Engel scale presented earlier in this chapter, there are not only events happening before a person joins the church, but there are several points that occur after conversion, if the person is truly to develop into a loving disciple of Jesus Christ. We spend a lot of money getting people into the church. Certainly it is worth following them through to make certain they develop relationships in the church and thus stay in the church.

## SUMMARY

This chapter has examined the whole concept of friendship evangelism as the ideal sowing and cultivating tool. The reader should remember that this alone will not give us a rich harvest—it must be combined with some reaping event. When sowing, cultivating, and reaping happen, churches flourish and grow.

All the evidence suggests the strong need to develop relationships with people as the foundation not only for winning people to Jesus, but for keeping them in the church after they join. In the next chapter, we will be exploring ways to help visitors feel more at home when they attend our churches. With members committed to friendship evangelism, the result will be a lot of visitors attending our churches. How can we make them feel comfortable?

## Notes:

1. White. *Ministry of Healing*, 143. Also, see Chapter 5.

2. Neighbors, Jr., Ralph W. *Future Church* (Nashville: Broadman Press, 1980), 163. Quoted by Win Arn. *The Master's Plan for Making Disciples* (Grand Rapids, MI: Baker Books, 1998), 37.

3. Acts 16:14, 15.

4. Luke 19:9.

5. Mark 5:1-20.

6. Sahlin, Monte. 1993 Unpublished data from a survey of members as part of the 1993 General Conference World Survey. Similar results were seen as reported by Roger Dudley in a 1980 survey, published in *Adventures in Church Growth* (Washington, D.C.: Review and Herald, 1983).

7. Arn. *The Master's Plan for Making Disciples.*

8.  White. *Ministry of Healing*, 143.

9.  Yeakley, Flavil R. "A Profile of the New Convert: Patterns of Dissatisfaction"; "A Profile of the New Convert: Change in Life Situation"; "Views of Evangelism"; in *The Pastor's Church Growth Handbook*, Volume II, edited by Win Arn (Pasadena, CA: Church Growth Press, 1982).

10.  Arn, Win. Leadership Seminar, "Discovering Lifestyle Evangelism" (Copyright Church Growth, Inc.), 5A.

11.  Wagner, C. Peter. *Strategies for Church Growth* (Ventura, CA: Regal Books, 1987), 124.

12.  Yeakley, Flavil R. *Church Growth: America* 7 (January, 1981): 10, 11.

13.  Fox, H. Eddie, and George Morris. *Faith-sharing: dynamic Christian witnessing by invitation* (Nashville, TN: Discipleship Resources, 1986), 79, 80.

14.  Ibid.

15.  Yeakley. "Views of Evangelism," in *The Pastor's Church Growth Handbook*, Volume II, edited by Win Arn, 144.

16.  Arn. Leadership Seminar, "Discovering Lifestyle Evangelism," 5B.

17.  Ibid., 5C.

18.  Burrill, Russell. *The Revolutionized Church of the Twenty-First Century* (Fallbrook, CA: Hart Research Center, 1997).

19.  Arn. Leadership Seminar, "Discovering Lifestyle Evangelism," 5C.

20.  Ibid.

# CHAPTER EIGHT

# Church Visitors

Churches that are reaching out to their neighbors with community involvement and friendship evangelism will discover a constant stream of visitors attending church Sabbath after Sabbath. Here are people who are not strangers to the church—they actually took the time to attend one of our worship services. Sometimes they are new believers checking us out; other times, they are new people who have just moved into the community and are checking out the local Adventist church.

Sometimes, we assume that because some are already Adventists moving into the area, they do not need special attention, such as a new convert does. However, the Adventist church loses a lot of people when they move to a new community. They don't fit into the new church. The people are not the same as in the old church. Soon, they may soon move into an inactive state and then exit the back door. Every Adventist church should be on the lookout for visitors, whether they be Adventists or not. Each visitor should be warmly welcomed and made to feel at home.

Traveling as much as I do, I frequently attend different churches. Sometimes, it seems as if I am attending a different Adventist church almost every week. Most of the churches I attend recognize me, because I am speaking there, so they give me attention as a visitor. That does not count. However, when I attend a church where I am not known, I get a better perception of how that church treats visitors. Let me illustrate by two true stories that happened to me.

I had an appointment in a large city on a Sunday. I flew into the city on Friday to avoid Sabbath travel and planned to attend one of the metropolitan churches on Sabbath morning. My plane was delayed, and I arrived just a few minutes before Sabbath, just in time to check into the hotel near the airport. As I pondered where I would attend church the next morning, I opened the telephone book and checked the listing for Adventist churches. There were multiple possibilities. I decided to attend one church that many had told me had become a very vibrant congregation.

Since I had made no provision for lunch, I was hopeful that the church would have a potluck, where I could obtain Sabbath lunch. I decided to go early, so that if there was no potluck listed in the bulletin, there would still be time to go to another church and try my luck there.

As I arrived at this vibrant church, it was evident that this was going to be an exciting experience. Even arriving early, there were already many people there. The church seated around 300, and by church time, it was full. As I walked into the foyer, I was warmly greeted by the hostess and made to feel welcome. I moved into the sanctuary and sat down, opened the bulletin, and was relieved to discover that they planned a potluck for this Sabbath.

The service proceeded with innovative worship. I glanced around me at the excited people in the congregation. You could see their happiness in Jesus on their faces. This, indeed, was a vibrant, energizing congregation. The sermon was excellent—the music was alive. The people sang with their whole heart. It was a joyful, happy experience.

But then the service ended. Even though the bulletin mentioned the potluck, nothing was ever said publicly. I wanted to go, but wished to be personally invited. When visiting churches, I like to act as if I'm a stranger who does not understand the protocol, so I can discover what the church is really like. Yet no one approached me to invite me. I made my way out to the foyer, where happy people were enjoying each other in different groups. As I made my way between the groups, no one seemed even to notice that I was there.

I walked back into the sanctuary and came out another door, where other groups were enjoying each others' fellowship, but the same indifference to me was manifested. Not to be discouraged, I interrupted one of them and asked where the restroom was. One person turned and pointed down the hall but never uttered a word. Of course, no one speaks to you in the restroom.

When I emerged from the restroom, the aroma of the Adventist pot-luck filled my nostrils, so I made my way down the hall and stood outside the fellowship hall, right in front of the door. I was directly in the way of anyone who wanted to enter, hoping that they would invite me to come inside. Person after person came up to the door, said "Excuse me," opened the door, and walked in—but no one spoke to me.

Finally, I opened the door and walked in. The room was nearly full. People were sitting around round tables, obviously enjoying each other's fellowship. I stood there for five minutes, hoping to be invited to sit at a table, but instead was totally ignored. Finally, I noticed one table where no one was sitting, so I went over and sat down by myself. As people continued to arrive, the room filled up. Finally, all the seats were taken, except at my table, where I continued to sit alone. Soon the door opened, and another couple came in, looked around, noticed the empty seats at my table, came over, and asked if the seats were taken. I smiled and said No, expecting them to sit down. Instead, they said "Thank you" and proceeded to take the chairs and move them to another table.

Soon, we were invited to go and get our food. I stood in the line, got my food, made my way back to my lonesome table and was enjoying a good meal. Then another couple approached me and asked, again, if the chairs were taken. I expected them to move the chairs somewhere else, but they sat down. As we began to talk, I discovered that they were visitors, too.

You may feel I am exaggerating. I am not. This actually happened to me in a church that outwardly appeared to be very vibrant. However, in reality, the vibrancy was just on the surface. Even though I enjoyed the worship, I would never attend that church again if I were back in that same metropolitan area. They were certainly not visitor-friendly. Yet, if you were to ask the members, they would most assuredly tell you that they are extremely friendly. And they *were* friendly—to themselves. A church cannot be the judge of how friendly it is—only the visitor can tell the truth.

Another time, the scenario was the same. Only the city was different. I went searching for a church and decided to attend a small one in the city. However, I was never able to locate it. Even though it was listed in the Yellow Pages, there was no sign or any indication of a church in that area. Even after asking local people, I was unable to find anyone who had even heard of the church. Maybe they met in a house or a rented building, I do not know. So, finally, I found another church—a large one in the city—and entered, hoping for the potluck. I was not to be disappointed, for a potluck was clearly marked in the bulletin.

When it was time to divide for Sabbath School classes, I anxiously remained seated to see what would happen. Quickly, someone came over and invited me to their class—a vibrant, exciting Sabbath School discussion. After the lesson, I quickly went back to my isolated pew, where I could see what was happening. As soon as I sat down, several people from the class came over and sat nearby and, again, welcomed me. I wondered if they would announce the potluck and invite the visitors. They did.

Of course, I hoped for a personal invitation. After the service, I headed for the back of the church. I was invited several times to come to the potluck in this 300-member congregation. I tried to go out the front door to place my Bible in the car before going to potluck, but they would hardly let me out without promising to come back in for lunch. I truly felt welcomed.

I finally arrived at the fellowship hall with all the round tables. I was warmly greeted. I proceeded to sit down at one of the empty tables. I was only there a minute, when a man from a nearby table came over and sat with me. He then spent the whole time eating with me and getting acquainted. Only at the end of the potluck did I realize that he had left his family at the other table.

Which church do you think I would join if I had to choose between the two? The first one had a more vibrant worship service, but no matter how boring the sermon might be (and it was not), I would still choose the second church because of the friendliness and warmth of the congregation.

Was this all planned? I do not know. It appeared spontaneous. Yet having worked so many years with churches, I know that such things don't just happen. I believe someone was in charge at the potluck to watch out for visitors and go sit with them. Such things do not happen without someone in charge. Visitor friendliness is never happenstance—it is always planned.

### WHY VISITORS RETURN TO A CHURCH

Several years ago Robert Bast[1] conducted research that indicated why visitors return to a church. The reasons were given in descending order of importance, but the first was very clear. The warmth and friendliness of the congregation is the primary reason people return to a given church. Therefore, a church that is serious about following up its visitors will make certain that plans are made to give specific attention to visitors. Sometimes churches think that because they are friendly "up front," that this can substitute for real caring in the aisles. It cannot.

Visitors do not want to be "made over." They don't crave public attention. But they do enjoy the personal attention of members. It is this that constitutes a friendly church. Official greeters do not count. There are two times on Sabbath morning when visitors are apt to feel awkward. Those times are when they first enter the building—and when the formal part of the service is over. The second time is the most neglected. This is when the members gather in their groups, and the visitors meander their way between the groups as they exit the church, never to return.

The first problem is handled well by good greeters stationed at all the entrances to the church. As I have visited churches, it is amazing to note how many do not have greeters. In some places, I walk in, and the bulletins are just sitting on a table for people to help themselves—but there is no human contact. I have attended countless churches where I never even received a handshake, though attending both Sabbath School and church.

Yet most churches do provide a greeter. Ideally, of course, the greeters are caring people who have a warm smile and a firm handshake. Sometimes the first thing the greeter says to a person after the greeting is to ask them to sign the guestbook. Here is an unchurched person who, with trepidation, has just entered an Adventist church for the first time. And within one minute of entering, the visitor is asked to sign something. It can be very frightening. We mean well, but signing guestbooks is really not visitor-friendly. It is all right to get their name and address, but that is better done a little later, rather than upon entry.

I suggest that during the announcement period, the pastor or elder could tell the visitors that the ushers will be going up the aisle with a packet of materials about the church. If they are a visitor, they should feel free to reach out and take one. In the packet is a registration card that they can be encouraged to fill out. You may not get as many names, but your visitors are more apt to return. It is strange—we work so hard to get the names of visitors when they enter, but few churches ever do anything with the names. Sign your name at an evangelistic meeting, and we will quickly be at your doorstep, but sign your name in a church guestbook, and nothing will ever happen. The visitor simply does not know that the guestbook is seldom followed up.

Ideally, as people enter, they are warmly greeted and given a bulletin. Then someone in the foyer just happens to overhear that they are a visitor and comes over and greets them, offers to show them where the children's Sabbath School is, invites them to their adult Sabbath School class, and sits with them at church. This scenario does not just happen. It is planned. Growing churches place such people as unofficial greeters in the foyer who watch for visitors. It appears to just happen, but it is all planned.

The other time it is very difficult for visitors is at the end of the worship service. As people mingle with their friends and engage in lively conversations, the new person feels out of place, since no one is talking to them. A good strategy would be to have several greeters (unofficial), who go to the foyer during the closing song (the exact number would depend on the size of the congregation). Their job would be to watch for visitors and engage them in conversation. However, they should also be instructed to watch for members no one is engaging in conversation. The job of these people is to make certain no one leaves church without feeling that they have friends in that church.

The second most important reason that visitors return is the character of the worship service. In my first story, the service was full of joy and excitement. The church met this test, but it failed the more important test of friendliness. What do we mean by the character of the worship service? Is the service filled with joy? We don't mean that everyone is laughing, but rather that there is holy joy in the presence of the Lord. The atmosphere will not appear to be like that of a funeral.

Grace must be not only heard in the sermon, it must be experienced by the people attending the service. Furthermore, participants in worship should reflect the ethnicity, the gender, and the ages of the congregation. Those who attend should quickly realize that this church is a place where they will feel included. If all the participants on the platform are old white men, a wrong signal is being sent to the newcomers—only old white men can do anything in this church.

The third area of concern is that the church is seen as a family place. This is especially true of young couples, who are looking for a church where not only their kids can get involved, but where there is a dynamic adult program that fits their needs. What is the church offering outside of Sabbath morning? Is the church a one-day-a-week kind of church, or are there regular activities outside of Sabbath morning?

The church building and its condition is another area of concern. First of all, is the church visible? If people can't find the church, they will never visit. Like the church in my second story, I was not even able to find the church, so I could not visit it. Some Adventist churches are so located that one would never be able to find them, even in the time of trouble! So make certain that your church has a good sign in front. See to it that it is listed in the Yellow Pages and that its website is up to date. Be sure that appropriate directional signs have been installed so that if he church is not on a main street, it can easily be found.

Is the church accessible? Do you know how to get into the building? Can handicapped people get in easily? You would be surprised at how difficult it is to get into some churches. I was speaking at a church one Sabbath morning. When I arrived, several cars were in the parking lot. I made my way to the front door, but it was locked. Knowing people were inside, I knocked. A voice from inside said to go around to the side. What a welcome! Imagine a visitor encountering that welcome. I would have gone back to my car and gone to another church if I hadn't been the speaker. When I got inside, I found they had barricaded the front door. All the members knew not to use that door, but I was a visitor, and there were no signs outside to let us know.

One church had two entries to the building. The original entry in the front where the main foyer was located and a back entry near the parking lot that entered into a smaller foyer. Members would enter the back entry, cross the small foyer, go outdoors and proceed to the main foyer in the front. There was also a door in this small foyer that opened into the front of the sanctuary, but it was usually closed, and members knew to not enter there when the service had started, but to go instead to the main foyer.

Visitors, of course, did not know that. They would see people entering the back door and figured that was the way to go. Yet when they stepped inside, there were no greeters. All the members knew the greeting was done in the main foyer in the front, but there were no signs telling people to go outside in order to get to the main foyer. They did notice a door, but when they opened it, they found themselves awkwardly standing in front of the entire congregation. This is not the way to welcome visitors.

What is the condition of the property of the church? Is it in good shape? Is it being kept up, or does it have a run-down look? I remember one church that had a fairly large hole in the carpet halfway down the center aisle. When the deacons came down the aisle, they carefully walked around the hole so they would not trip. When I enquired how long the hole had been there, I discovered it had existed for three years or more. The members just did not see the need of replacing the carpet for one hole in the center aisle!

A run-down facility indicates a church with low morale. Newcomers are not interested in joining a church that does not appreciate its facility enough to keep it in good repair. Since the woman is the one who usually makes the decision to return to a church, it is especially important that the women's restroom, kitchen, and nursery all be in top shape. You can get by with a poor men's room, but not an out-of-date ladies' room. Do not have the grandmothers design the nursery. Things have changed since they had babies. Make certain that current mothers have a say in what is needed.

Finally, the church's image in the community is a factor in whether visitors attend. A church can improve its image through community service activities. When members and the pastor belong to various groups in the community, it builds relationships that result in people from the community visiting your church.

## FOLLOWING UP VISITORS

After the visitor leaves, what should the church do? Most churches do nothing and just hope the visitor will return. Churches that follow up visitors usually visit or call the visitor within forty-eight hours. (It is highly recommended that this visit be done by telephone rather than in person.) This is just a brief call to let the visitor know that the church appreciated their presence and ask if there is anything more the church can do to help them. The purpose of the visit is just to get acquainted and to encourage the visitor to return a second time. One should not usually attempt to evangelize on this visit, if the visitor is not an Adventist.

If the visitor returns, a second visit should be made, preferably by lay people of similar age. An elderly couple visiting a young family would not be the ideal match, since we are hoping for a relationship to form, even at this early stage of their involvement in the church. During this visit, the lay person should encourage the newcomer to get involved in some of the activities of the church. If they sing, invite them to join the choir. If they have children, get them into Pathfinders. If they are interested in a small group, suggest one where they could quickly get involved. The whole purpose here is to fellowship them. If they are not Adventists, one might, at this point, suggest Bible studies. Again, the purpose is to fellowship them and keep them coming.

Remember that people need relational bonding before they feel they are part of a church. This is true whether the people are not yet believers or if they are Adventists transferring from another church. We need to get beyond the idea that the only thing important in joining the church is knowing the doctrines. As important as doctrines are, they can never be a substitute for fellowship. The early New Testament church was powerful, not just because its members had seen the risen Christ but also because, Scripture declares, their fellowship was deep. Daily, they broke bread together, prayed together, studied the Bible together, and sang together. The emphasis was on fellowship.

My wife and I had just moved to Berrien Springs, Michigan, to begin our work there. We arrived on December 23. Christmas that year was on a Friday. We spent Christmas unpacking and then went to church at the large campus church—Pioneer Memorial Church. We were invited to sign a guest card, which we did. Sabbath afternoon we were sitting in our new home, boxes everywhere, when a knock came at the door. When we opened it, we found a couple from the church, coming to welcome us to the community.

As we talked, I discovered that they did not know that we were new faculty coming to Andrews. They thought we might have been students, but they visited us anyway, because that was important, even if it was Christmas weekend. That deeply impressed me and my wife. Today we are members of the Pioneer Memorial Church. My initial thought on moving to Berrien Springs was to join a small church, but the friendliness manifested to us on arrival made all the difference.

Did that just happen? No, obviously, it was planned. Remember, friendliness and warmth must be worked on. It never happens all on its own. With careful planning and a well-thought-out strategy, your church can have an excellent program in place so that visitors are not neglected but made to feel a real part of the community of faith. Why not share this chapter with your greeting committee and see if some of the strategic ideas suggested might be implemented in your church? It might just result in more visitors attending.

## Things Held in Common by Churches Attracting Visitors

In Robert Bast's book, he also enumerates five issues held in common by churches that are good in attracting visitors.[2] A quick look at them will conclude this chapter.

These churches above all have a positive identity and good self-image. Churches that are attracting visitors feel good about themselves. They are proud of their church. When members are ashamed of how the church looks, or uncomfortable with what happens on Sabbath morning, or fearful that the wrong thing will be said up front, they will not invite their friends to come to church with them. However, members who are excited about what is happening at their church will constantly be bringing their friends and neighbors to experience the joy they are finding.

The second area is that of congregational harmony. Churches that are fighting rarely attract or keep visitors coming. When the word is out that you are welcome here, but only if you join "our" side, few people will return. The conflict does not even need to be visible. When a church is in conflict, you can sense it in the atmosphere of the church. So solve the conflict and get back to sharing the good news of Jesus.

The third area is pastoral enthusiasm. Is the pastor exciting to be around? Does he make the sermon interesting, or is he so dry that the members are falling asleep during the sermon? Rarely do people decide to attend a church because of the pastor, but many times they will decide never to return because of the pastor. The pastor does not need to be an entertainer, but the delivery and content of the message needs to be such that it feeds the souls of those who attend.

The fourth area is the church's ministry in the community. How active is the church in community activities? Does it do things for the community, or it is only a leech, taking out of the community but never putting anything back in? We have already discussed community involvement in this book, but it is added here simply for emphasis on its importance.

The final component that churches attracting visitors have in common is small group activities. Again, we have talked considerably about this issue. This is really critical for newcomers, for the small group provides them an opportunity to get acquainted. Rarely does one build relationships simply by attending church on Sabbath morning. Small groups provide time for face-to-face relational building.

## SUMMARY

Churches that are growing, vibrant Adventist congregations in the twenty-first century will not only be reaching out through friendship evangelism but will see many of the contacts made in the community developing into people who visit the church. After they attend once or twice, they are no longer guests or visitors—they have become regular attenders and should no longer be referred to as visitors. Imagine how it would feel if you had attended a church for six months, but they still called you a visitor just because your name had not yet been added to the roles. Churches should focus on inclusiveness rather than exclusiveness. When visitors attend, they are cared for in these growing, vibrant Adventist churches. As a result, first- and second-time visitors quickly emerge as regular attenders, and ultimately, the regular attenders transform into dynamic new Adventists.

**Notes:**

1. Bast, Robert. *Attracting New Members* (New York, NY and Monrovia, CA: Co-published by Reformed Church in America and Church Growth, Inc., 1988).

2. Ibid.

# CHAPTER NINE

# Discipleship

You have just concluded an evangelistic series in your church, during which thirty-five precious people were baptized and joined the church. The whole church is reveling in the excitement of these new faces. Vibrancy is the only way to describe what the church is experiencing during this exciting time. Now the meetings are over. The people in the church are tired. They are ready to get back to life as normal in the church. However, remember that normalcy, for many churches, is disobedience to Christ.

Just because people are baptized does not mean that your work is done. In fact, it is just the beginning. The commission of Jesus was not for the church to go forth and get baptisms, but rather to make disciples (Matthew 28:19). Discipleship actually begins before the people are baptized, but there is also a lot of work to do after they are baptized. In this chapter we wish to address the issues of discipleship that occur primarily after a person is baptized.

My book, *Radical Disciples for Revolutionary Churches*[1] takes a serious look at the issue of discipleship. While there may be some redundancy here with that work, I would like briefly to share some of those concepts, plus new ideas I have learned since then. For detailed information, the reader is referred to *Radical Disciples for Revolutionary Churches*.

Any discipleship plan must be built around the discipleship model of Jesus. He is the One who commanded His followers to go forth and make disciples. As we examine the gospels, we discover five passages in which Jesus defines a disciple. We will examine those five passages and then seek to develop our discipleship model around the definition Jesus established.

A disciple is not above his master, nor the servant above his lord. It is enough for the disciple that he be as his master, and the servant as his lord. If they have called the master of the house Beelzebub, how much more shall they call them of his household?[2]

In this passage Jesus is not declaring that a disciple cannot be above the master in a hierarchical system, but instead is declaring that disciples will experience the same treatment that Jesus received. If the devil was angry with Jesus, he will be angry with the followers of Jesus. Persecution and ridicule have been the lot of the disciples of Jesus since the inception of Christianity. It will be no different today. Part of being a follower of Christ is to expect hostility.

Christ did not call His followers to a life of ease. Throughout history, genuine Christianity has repeatedly experienced times of persecution and ridicule. God has never promised a prosperity gospel. Such a gospel is totally foreign to the first-century Jesus. Yet Christians are also not to develop a persecution complex, whereby they invite persecution.

If hardship is part of the Christian paradigm, then when we disciple people, we must help them develop a faith maturity that will enable them to withstand the persecution and ridicule that will come upon those who profess to be followers of the meek and mild Jesus. Churches cannot leave people in Christianity 101 or even Adventism 101. To disciple, by this definition, means to help people develop faith maturity. What are you doing in your church to help new Adventists develop faith maturity?

If any man come to me, and hate not his father, and mother, and wife, and children, and brethren, and sisters, yea, and his own life also, he cannot be my disciple. And whosoever doth not bear his cross, and come after me, cannot be my disciple.

So likewise, whosoever he be of you that forsaketh not all that he hath, he cannot be my disciple.[3]

The call of the Master overpowers everything else in one's life. Jesus uses the word *hate* here as an Oriental hyperbole, meaning "to love less." The essence of this definition of discipleship is that a disciple is one who has Jesus as the top priority of life. Nothing surpasses or comes between the believer and God. This is very high commitment.

The call to discipleship is not for half-hearted people—the call is for a radical commitment of one's life to Jesus. No other person or thing can stand in the way of one's radical commitment to Christ. Sometimes today we seem to try to lessen the minimum qualifications, to make it easier for people to join. Jesus never did that. He raised the standard high. Nothing less than total commitment was the basic entry level for Christianity.

Today we sometimes confuse raising the standards with lifestyle issues, but Jesus' standard rises far above such miniscule earthly standards. Jesus is examining the heart. He is seeking to bring out a people who live in a radical commitment to Him in every area of their lives—not just in the externals. Jesus is far more interested in what is occurring in the heart than in what is happening on the outside of one's life.

One cannot be Jesus' disciple by just obeying a few rules that the church might impose. One becomes a disciple as one allows Jesus to have absolute control of every area of one's life. Nothing is exempt from the demand of the cross. This commitment is much stronger than any lifestyle commitment we may make. In fact, many people who conform to the outward, external rules may not even faintly represent the height of commitment demanded by Jesus. The cost of discipleship is internal, not just external. Of course, when one has the internal commitment, there will also be evidence in the externals of one's life, but we should never confuse the two. It is always possible to have external commitment, but not internal. Yet one cannot have internal commitment without external evidence.

> Jesus therefore was saying to those Jews who had believed Him, If you abide in My word, then you are truly disciples of Mine; and you shall know the truth, and the truth shall make you free.[4]

This third passage defining a disciple points to the very heart of discipleship—a living relationship with the risen Lord. It is not enough to know the basic teachings of Jesus—one must also know Him. Scripture truth is not for the sake of cognitive recognition, but such knowledge must lead to a living relationship with Christ. Therefore, part of the discipleship process is to help people learn how to study the Bible and pray so that they develop this dynamic relationship.

Astonishingly, most churches assume that new converts know how to do this. This may have been true in past generations, when the majority of people who joined the Seventh-day Adventist Church came from another denomination, but today most folk join from an unchurched background. They know nothing about how to pray or study the Bible for spiritual strength.

Sadly, many Adventists do not themselves spend quality time with God daily. Many do not even bring their Bibles to church. We even provide them a Bible in the pew, so they do not need to bring theirs, or we put the text on the screen, so they do not even have to look it up. The result is that many Adventists are biblically illiterate today.

Jesus indicates that a disciple is one who has gone deep into the Word of God. The person knows God, communicates with Him through prayer and Bible study, and this communication results in a dynamic, living relationship with Jesus. What are you doing in your church for your new converts to make certain they learn how to study the Bible and pray? What are you doing to help them make this relationship real in their life?

> By this all men will know that you are My disciples, if you have love for one another.[5]

Jesus is clear. Love is the crowning evidence of discipleship. To discover who the real people of God are, Jesus declares that we need to find a people who love each other. How contrary that is to what we sometimes tell new converts: "You have found the perfect message, but watch out for the people. Don't look at the people. Keep your eyes on Jesus."

It is difficult to argue with those statements, except that theologically they are totally wrong and the opposite of what Jesus said here. Jesus declares that we *are* to look to the people and find that His disciples will be known for how much they love. Perhaps it is time we stop excusing our lack of love under the umbrella of "we have the truth." If we have the truth, we will love. The love spoken here is the *agape* unselfish love displayed by Jesus when He gave His life for us. That same love will be found among Christ's followers—or they are not His disciples. Strong words, but they are not mine—they belong to Jesus.

I just received a Christmas card from a person who attended our most recent evangelistic series. They were not baptized in the meeting, but have been attending ever since the meeting. This is what the wife wrote to me:

We have just sent a letter, dissolving our membership to our previous church. We will be joyfully joining the Seventh Day Church very shortly. The love we have experienced is what Jesus wants all His children to give and receive. We visited a Seventh Day church in the mountains and experienced the same love. The Word of God is alive in this church. We are excited to be a part of this family.

She is right. It was not the truth that won her to Adventism. It was the love she experienced in the family of God. What are you doing to manifest that love in your church, and what preparation are you making to ensure that new converts also develop this same love?

By this is My Father glorified, that you bear much fruit, and so prove to be My disciples.[6]

Jesus' disciples will be fruit producers. What is the fruit that disciples produce? More disciples. In the context of this passage Jesus is clearly showcasing the reproductive function of His disciples. If one is not reproducing, one is not a disciple of Jesus. Look at the context of this passage.

These things I have spoken to you, that My joy may be in you, and that your joy may be made full.[7]

You did not choose Me, but I chose you, and appointed you, that you should go and bear fruit, and that your fruit should remain, that whatever you ask of the father My name, He may give to you.[8]

The joy of Jesus, the joy of the apostle Paul, was seeing souls in the kingdom of God.[9] For this Jesus endured the cross and Paul endured persecution. Clearly, the context here is that fruit is the creation of new disciples. A disciple is a disciple maker.

No sooner is one converted than there is born within him a desire to make known to others what a precious friend he has found in Jesus. The saving and sanctifying truth cannot be shut up in his heart.[10]

Every true disciple is born into the kingdom of God as a missionary.[11]

Our work in discipleship is not complete until the new convert is reaching out and winning new people to Jesus. The reproductive cycle is part of the discipleship process. Note that Jesus also indicates that it is not occasional fruit, but "much fruit" and that the "fruit will remain." The life of the disciple of Jesus is one of constant fruit-picking for the kingdom. What are you doing in your church to make certain new converts enter into a lifestyle of evangelism and disciple making?

## CREATING AN ADVENTIST DISCIPLESHIP MODEL

The Adventist Church today needs to develop a holistic strategy for discipleship. We do a very good job of getting people onto the membership roles and retaining them in the pew. However, discipleship, as we have seen, is deeper than agreeing to twenty-eight cognitive truths and then sitting in a pew for the rest of one's life. It is a radical commitment of the whole life to the radical Jesus. Jesus' definition of disciple must form the basis for any discipleship plan your church develops.

In this section, I wish to share a few thoughts on four basic areas the church must focus on if it is to make disciples after the definition of Jesus. As your church seeks to develop a discipleship plan, it would be wise to build it around the areas we are suggesting. There may be other areas that will need attention, but these are certainly the basics that must be considered in developing a plan.


### 1. Getting people into membership.

This area is one that Adventists have already thoroughly developed. In most churches, not much work is needed here. We do an excellent job of reaching people initially, but it is what we fail to do after they join the church that creates problems for Adventists. In order to get people into membership, we must first of all help them to accept Jesus Christ as their personal Savior. One cannot be a church member if one has not surrendered one's life to Jesus. The person should also be committed to making Jesus Lord of their life, and there ought to be some tangible evidence that Lordship has begun to happen. Keeping Sabbath, paying tithe, practicing good health would certainly be evidences that a person is beginning to make Jesus Lord of their life, not only in word but also in deed. Furthermore, as Adventists, we would expect that such people are acquainted with and understand the twenty-eight fundamental beliefs of the Adventist Church.

Those would be the basic issues that are covered in the process of becoming a Seventh-day Adventist. Most evangelists do an excellent job here. Of the four areas we are dealing with, this first step is the one that is most developed in the Adventist Church; however, we might need to hone the skill a little, especially in the area of connecting lifestyle issues to a relationship with Jesus as Lord of one's life.

### 2. Becoming a mature spiritual person in Christ.

Of all the issues we are dealing with in discipleship, my personal opinion is that this area is our greatest need. People may have cognitive belief, but it is not transferring into spirituality. A spiritual person is by definition one who has a dynamic, living relationship with the risen Christ.

Relationships only develop when people spend time with Jesus. What mechanism does your church have in place to teach people how to study the Bible and how to pray? These essential spiritual disciplines are totally neglected in most Adventist churches. We baptize people who believe the message, but we fail to help them learn how to study on their own.

Perhaps this is because in ages past most people joined Adventism through another Christian walk, and we assumed they knew how to pray and how to study for spiritual growth. However, with people primarily joining us from an unchurched background today, this education has become an absolute necessity. We must do more than admonish them to pray and study. They will take our admonition, begin reading Genesis, and get lost somewhere halfway through Exodus. What courses are offered by your church to help people learn to pray to God as a friend? Are there courses on how to study the Bible? I am not talking about a Bible study, but learning how to use the concordance, and how to study the Bible for personal spiritual growth. When all we do is admonish but do not provide step-by-step instruction, most people give up and join the ranks of their fellow biblically illiterate church members. They may even come to Sabbath School weekly and offer their opinion, as they see other church members doing, rather than share their biblical insights gained from personal study of the Word. Sadly, in many Adventist Sabbath Schools today, the members just share their collective biblical illiteracy.

Becoming a spiritual person also means to learn how to love and care with the *agape* love of Jesus. This is the part that especially characterizes the disciple, according to Jesus' definition. Love and care come naturally from personal Bible study and prayer. Communion with God and His Word always produces the fruit of the Spirit in the lives of transformed people.

However, it is not enough to know about love; one must also be able to demonstrate that love. This is why involvement in a small group is so essential as part of the discipleship process. There, people can learn how to manifest the love of Jesus, for they will see it in action in their fellow small group leaders. These small groups cannot be cognitive only—they must also be relational. Knowledge must be placed into action, or it is worthless. Perhaps this is why we have discovered that rarely, if ever, do we lose a new member who joins a small group.

The small relational group provides a place where people can grow in their spiritual life with support from fellow travelers on life's spiritual journey. Here they can hold each other accountable for their life in Christ. Here is a place truly to manifest the fulfillment of all the "one another" passages in the New Testament describing members caring for each other.

Amazingly, in spite of the overwhelming endorsement of small groups by Ellen White[12] and the demonstration of vitality that is happening in Adventist churches that practice holistic small groups, many Adventists vehemently reject participation in small groups. They do so to their own detriment. One cannot invite new people to join a group, if one is not in a group. Yet Holistic Small Groups remains the worst-developed characteristic in Adventist churches that utilize the Natural Church Development system of church health. In developing a discipleship plan for your church, consider how you can get more church members involved in small groups in your church. How can you ensure that all new members join a small group? If you are serious about discipleship, your church will tackle this neglected area.

### 3. Getting people into ministry.

People who are discipled will be involved in ministry. I have written much about the great need for every member to be a minister. I do not intend to repeat all that here. I bring it up simply to indicate, once again, the absolute necessity for involving people in ministry as soon as they become members, and, in some cases, before their name even makes it onto the books of the church.

As soon as people join the church and enter the discipleship process, other members should begin to help them discover their spiritual gifts and their place of ministry in the body of Christ. Obviously, the best place for this to occur is in a holistic small group. When spiritual gift discovery occurs apart from a small group, people rarely utilize their gift, but when discovered as part of the expectation of group involvement, they usually end up in a gift-based ministry.

There is a difference between knowing one's spiritual gift and actual involvement in ministry in harmony with one's gift. In the Natural Church Development process we have discovered that the problem in Adventism generally is not the system of discovering one's gift, but instead, it is actual deployment into a ministry in harmony with one's gift. Somehow it all breaks down between the discovery of a gift and the time one gets put into ministry. What is your church doing to help new and existing members become involved in a ministry that is in harmony with their giftedness?

Ministry involvement is not an option for Christians. The Bible is clear that we are all priests to Christ, and as His priests, we have a ministry. The question should never be raised as to whether a person desires to get into ministry. The expectation should be that all will be involved. The only question is which ministry the member will be involved in. To fail to be involved in a ministry is disobedience to Jesus, and that is intolerable for Adventist Christians.

### 4. Becoming a missionary person.

The final area with which the discipleship process should concern itself is helping the new disciple to discover their reproductive function. Again, involvement in sharing one's faith is not optional, as mentioned earlier. What needs to happen here is not simply admonishing new people to share their faith, but helping them to make witnessing a part of their lifestyle.

Many new people immediately turn off their families to Adventism. They hear about the mark of the beast and go quickly and share it with their Catholic grandmother. Then they wonder why their family is so difficult to reach. You must get to new people quickly and help them understand that they must let their family see what a difference this new faith has made in their lives, rather than diving into the more advanced information. This will help family members develop a desire to begin the process of learning how this message made such a significant, positive change in their relative's life.

Another area of instruction and training is helping the new person identify the people in their extended family who are open to the faith and showing them how to begin sharing Jesus with these relatives in a non-threatening way. Helping new people learn how to share the beautiful truth of Jesus with people at their workplace also requires training and counsel.

As people are discipled, they will better know how to help disciple others. Our current problem stems from the fact that most existing members were never fully discipled—only brought into membership. Somehow, this false cycle has to be changed so that people will truly become disciples of Jesus.

These four areas are the essential ingredients of a good discipleship program operating in the local church. Examine your structure and your plans. Are you currently leading people through all four areas, or are you just making church members? Don't get overly concerned if you are unable immediately to implement all four areas. Develop one area well, and then begin working on another.

Obviously, to move to discipleship instead of membership means that you will need to involve more of your present members in ministry. This is a positive result. Please do not try to add all this work onto the backs of those already involved in ministry, or you will burn them out. Utilize new people and get them involved in making disciples. In the process, they too will become discipled.

The ultimate goal is for people to be discipled in all four areas. When that occurs, your church will soar for God and truly fulfill the great commission to go forth and make disciples of all nations.

## Notes:

1. Burrill, Russell. *Radical Disciples for Revolutionary Churches* (Fallbrook, CA: Hart Research Center, 1996).

2. Matthew 10:24, 25, KJV.

3. Luke 14: 26, 27, 33, KJV.

4. John 8:31, 32, NASB.

5. John 13:35, NASB.

6. John 15:8, NASB.

7. John 15:11, NASB.

8. John 15:16, NASB.

9. Hebrews 12:2; 1 Thessalonians 2:19.

10. White, *Desire of Ages*, 141.

11. Ibid., 195.

12. White, *Testimonies for the Church*, vol. 7, 21.

# Epilogue

Growing Adventist churches and making disciples is the fulfillment of the mission of Jesus. In this book we have listed some simple principles that, when followed, will result in spontaneous growth of Adventist churches everywhere. Some may have preferred that I give a more detailed plan. Yet, I have discovered through the years that when churches work out the details on their own, they buy into the process more effectively, and the results are transformational. This is why I prefer to stick to principles that will apply broadly to all churches.

You have read the book, and now it is time to stop reading and go into action. Sit down with the church board and discuss what you have learned. Perhaps you will even want to share copies of this book with church board members. The next step is to move from discussion to the creation of action plans that will put into practice the principles outlined in this book, so that your church might live up to Christ's expectations for His people.

Remember, it is God's will that the church grow. He did not call us to failure but to success. It is His desire that all people come to the knowledge of God. It is His passion to enter into a relationship with all of humanity. He could have chosen angels to carry forward this work, but, amazingly, He has entrusted it to His church—the members of His body. We must stop living in sin and become the obedient people of God by going forth and fulfilling the great commission. So go, in His name, and make disciples—now.